I AM A SEEKER AND MY SEARCH GOES ON...

Kusum Ansal

Vitasta
Let Knowledge Spread

Published by
Renu Kaul Verma
Vitasta Publishing Pvt Ltd
2/15, Ansari Road, Daryaganj
New Delhi - 110 002
info@vitastapublishing.com

ISBN 9789386473028

First published in 1993 as *Sheltering Shadows* by Har Anand Publications

Cover and layout by Vits Press
Printed by Vikas Computer and Printers

The sky is beautiful, but abstract
far away and distant
But he is an earthly man
Simple yet gracious...
To Sushil Ji

Kusum

THE FIRST DAY of the Almanac or new year is never like all the other days that follow—at least not for me. As I opened my window, a strange nascent aroma of freshness wafts up from the pinnacles of fur and pine trees. A few sunrays, mysterious and diffused, seep through my window like a faint cloud. There were hazy shadows lurking in the corners of the garden. Perhaps that was the unknown, the new day, bringing with it a whole new year. Suddenly, I felt that the first day of the unseen masked new year was resting its head on my window sill, bursting to climb in. I realized it was not a normal day, it was something which was abstract and unknown, which was slowly becoming more tangible and physical. Yesterday was already last year.

The flowing winds of time have eroded a large segment of my life. The past, for me, has been strange, uncertain, and to a great extent unwanted. Everything in my life happened so abruptly that I lost faith in a predetermined pattern of life. Events do help in the metamorphosis of our very existence. Like the Roman priest who concealed messages in the folds of his long black robe, our future is also wrapped in an unseen mysterious robe of time. Time has no relationship with understanding, but time can help one to mature. Time helps one to attain the capacity to think, to think freely without fear, so that you begin to discover for yourself what is real and what is true. For me, the New Year day is different—it is a day of self-analysis and introspection. On this day I detatch myself from the present to look back into the past, and even visualize the future with some kind of hope and curiosity. The past has been strange, yet it has made me what I am, and has enriched my life.

The sun that morning appeared after a long and oppressively heavy snowfall. It is paradoxical that we feel the cold not when it snows but when the sky clears out. I had opened the window—melting snow flakes dripped down the tender branches of the pine and eucalyptus trees—a golden orange hue had magically transformed the surroundings into a heavenly sojourn that exuded divinity.

Mother and Pierre had danced till late last night—the melodious notes seemed to flow out of the heart—the pleasant breeze enveloping them seemed charged with their fervour. Mother was lost to the lilt of the music—memories had been pushed back to the unconscious mind.

A comprehensive analysis of memories has the potential to alter one's life and is hence perceived as being dangerous. The day to come was the day Papa had left her bereft of all music and happiness—probably that was the reason she revelled in this day.

Professor Sharatji and Naina were also busy dancing. Sharatji had not given me a second look after he was introduced to Naina. Perhaps I did not possess the requisite qualities to be called attractive.

"Can I get you some wine?" Sharatji whispered in Naina's ear.

"No thank you, I do not drink."

"Kebabs?"

"No, I am a vegetarian."

"How about a dance?"

"No, not even that."

"Then..."

"Then, go to hell," Naina said. They both laughed and Sharatji abruptly caught Naina's arm and whirled her on to the floor.

I wondered how I appeared to people. I remembered Naina saying, "How does one define you, Malvika? The eternal martyr—self suffering—why do you have such despair on your face ? Why can't you live life, each day as it comes—I don't know what affliction you suffer, as if a nail of the Cross has been hammered into you. Why don't you let yourself go—when was the last time you had a good laugh Malvika?"

There was no one at my table—only the twinkling bulbs intermittently dripping a diffused light. At that moment too, I had detached myself from the inconsequential events and needs of the night and pondered what configuration the new year would take. On looking back, there was Papa's death...Bhupen... Savita...desire...a home slipping away—this existence seemed unending...the contingent events, the pain, the success and failure—the intensities of drama played in the stormy recesses of the heart. But, mercifully, these storms calm down by the time they reach the conscious self. I often try with courage to descend to the dark anteroom of my vanquished desires, where a stench of my broken dreams and my parents' neglect are carefully stacked, and overawed sentiments, trodden memories await uncertainly to be locked into the dungeons of the mind.

Mother did not express anything in the morning. She had even forgotten the ceremony ritually held for the peace of the departed soul. I could hear the strains of the wakened morning—a clattering—the odds and ends of the party being cleared. Janaki, the housemaid with her grumbling, Bedi and his tirades. But the scene outside the window remained quiet and the guests continued to sleep. I had a strange desire to hear what Mother was saying. What a lot of deciphering, of the unsaid there is, in hearing. At the juncture where the mind goes beyond hearing and pauses, an opinion of what was heard is formed. I waited at just such a juncture—but Mother's words carried nothing but a wordliness about them. The only significant act of the day was to clear the trappings of last night's revelry—the bar glasses, the napkins, the streamers, the broken stars and spangles, the deflated balloons—yesterday's festoons had become today's debris. Mother saw me and said, "Are you going to college?"

"No, not immediately."

"Then please take this register and make an inventory of the whisky, wines and soda bottles."

"Oh, Mother," I objected, "not so early in the morning."

"There is no morning or evening in work. Besides, today is the First—there's so much to be done."

"Like what?" I asked in eager anticipation.

Perhaps she remembered.

"The routine—the servants' salaries, special tips for the new year—the washerman will soon be here."

I looked away…What does one do with a memory that does not have even a whisp of the fragrance of the old days. Mother said, "Malvika, please open the curtains, let's have a bit of light. Don't you think this was the first really exciting New Year's Eve celebration, here at Nirmal Kunj?"

"Well…may be…" I hesitated.

"Please draw the curtains. Don't you think these new curtains look beautiful?"

"Why do we put up curtains mother?"

"To furnish the room, and be protected against the strong glare."

"Protected against the glare or our reality?"

"You're speaking in Bhaiji's language again. Please spare me your philosophical ramblings." I thought it best to leave the room but was accosted by the sentry… "Maaji, the priest has come."

"How many times must I tell you not to call me Maaji—do I look a Mother—Can't you address me as Memsahib?"

"Yes Memsahib, the priest…"

"Yes, the priest. Must have come to collect his new year tips. It must be that boy from the shrine in the cave. Malvika, please give him something."

My uncertain steps led me to the priest—Roshanji. I invited him to be seated, organised the pooja and performed it all by myself. Papa's photograph and I—a few flowers, the chantings, and invocations—this was all that was left of relationships. Roshanji did not ask for Mother and I did not volunteer any explanations. When mother finally made an appearance, everything was over. Janaki appeared with a glass of milk and some breakfast for Roshanji. Mother was more angry than embarrassed..."You could have reminded me, if I forgot."

"Why remind you of something you've forgotten."

"Malvika...you have wrong notions about me."

"There is no right or wrong, Mother. We progressively respond to the state of our mind. My relationship with Papa is one of birth—that is truth and therefore, 'right'. An Indian sentiment, as Pierre would say."

Mother turned abruptly away. Perhaps I should not have mentioned Pierre's name—he was responsible for her attitude, for the change in her—but why did Mother always live outside herself. Why did she never indulge in self-realization?

I am constantly drudging at maintaining Nirmal Kunj. Mother's high pitched plea resounded in the room. She was right of course. Mother and I were both fettered to Nirmal Kunj. Some of the wings of the mansion had been left locked. Tourists came and went; and Mother and I went through the chores of looking after them meticulously. Yet, we could not imagine life without the tourists—they were like an addiction to us—our very subsistence. After Papa's death, it was this definite means which had made our capsized lives more worthwhile. I don't know which one of the two of us had been more affected by the disaster life had bestowed upon us.

***

ANY ATTEMPT AT recounting the truth is immediately accompanied by half truths, hidden truths and lies, and yet we never tire of believing the hollow sounds of our words. Our greatest problem I think is to accurately discern our own values. Mother was used to flamboyant luxury. Papa had been a very high government official, and the orderlies and servants had kept her busy with the showmanship of status. Her day started with being preoccupied with Papa, then sprucing up the house, the afternoon nap and later, the animated preparations for the evening's cocktails or dinner. I figured nowhere in her scheme of things. I lived with a governess, who looked after my needs and comforts very efficiently and with clockwork precision—but with little room for love. My childhood was a walk through dry sands, culminating in a thorny undergrowth of emotions. My existence in my parents' life was a negation in terms. I was their only child and hence a vital part of the household, but my presence did not arouse any possessiveness in them. They were so lost in a reckless celebration of life that they did not even pause to seek any of life's truths. They had the aptitude to ignore with ease, the indefinable yearning and pain that comes with growing up. My body was changing—I had changed from school to college. Change brings with it newness and sometimes maturity but not necessarily fulfilment. Neither an attempt at sentimentality nor material gain can ever make us feel complete. That was probably the reason why I found solace in books.They were certainly more entertaining than Mother's parties.

Bhaiji, Papa's elder brother, used to visit us sometimes. Papa or Mother never felt the need to rebuke me about anything. But, Bhaiji often exercised his rights as an elder, and admonished me. He would be annoyed with Mother's ways and express his disapproval to me.

"Your Mother hasn't perpetuated any traditions. You don't seem to know a single hymn or prayer."

"Bhaiji, does Mother know any?"

"That's the pity. A restless soul—always on the move, she's constantly spinning like a top."

I could not help laughing. This candid observation of mother was rather appealing. I knew he was worried about her. I wanted to please him—the one person who was concerned enough to scold me.

"Bhaiji, why don't you teach me some mantras and prayers?"

"I would, if I were to stay with you. I will send you a book on everyday prayer and ritual. Learn it up. Every girl should be religious."

"But isn't it more important to be human than religious? Are all religious people good?"

Bhaiji said affectionately, "Well, prayer increases our proximity to God. It's a way of disciplining and dedicating ourselves to him."

I would get influenced by all that Bhaiji said and I soon found myself learning up a lot of mantras and practising religious rituals whenever I could. I started believing that the chanting of prayers was the only act that would cleanse my soul. The incantations became a spontaneous inspiration to my consciousness. Whenever I felt lifeless and inconsequential, a small ember of the holy fire would glow inside me and the void inside would be filled with a strange tangible strength. The prayer books sent by Bhaiji and my graduation text books would fill the silence of the house.

My love for literature led me to Bhupen's novel and then finally to Bhupen. My best and only friend Savita was well groomed and bubbling with life. We would often discuss the future when we sat in a group with our other classmates. Once Savita said, "Come on girls, let's make a list of the qualities a boyfriend should possess."

Savita started reading the lists.

"Wanted, a hundred percent male, who possesses manly qualities…

"Is full of wisdom…"

"Has social graces and a sense of humour…"

"And interest in art and music…"

She paused as she came to my list. "A hundred percent male—should be religious. I think Malvika wants a priest or maybe a mendicant. Are you planning to get married or renounce the world?"

There were guffaws of laughter and I started wondering why I had written that. Why had I thought of a hundred percent man? Did this kind of a man exist in this world?

Around that time, Bhupen, won an award for his novel, and the college Dramatics Society brought out a dramatised version of it. Everything was so new and rain kissed—the play, acting and my acquaintance with Bhupen. I shall never forget those lovely days—a host of new friends—Mohan, Jivesh and Kanta. We would rehearse the entire day till late in the evenings.

Rakhakriti was the story of how declining relationships take their toll on the human psyche. It was the story of an ill-matched couple. The husband, a product of British education, denigrates everything Indian and looks upon India as unprogressive and stale. The wife is unable to change her Indian attitudes and values.

They both carry on living under the same roof because the husband cannot do without the luxuries that his wife's property and flourishing business provide him; and the wife, of course, is wedded to him and also to the traditions instilled in her from childhood. But she develops inscrutable ailments which doctors are unable to diagnose. She suffers alone—because during the course of her prolonged illness, everyone leaves her. The Visitor's Book lying outside her room is dutifully filled in by all her close friends and relatives who do not take the effort to step beyond the closed sickroom door. Her own sister, too, prefers to register her atttendance by merely signing the book.

The lady is shocked by such apathetic behaviour and requests her doctors to transfer her to a general ward of an ordinary hospital. She sees other human beings suffering more than herself. They are in pain—but not at all lonely. Loneliness is the cross she has to bear. She compares herself to a pencil sketch—a Rekhakriti. She has all the comforts of life but not affection with which to colour them. Who could portray loneliness better than Malvika? And I did—because for me the play was very symbolic and ironical. My parents had no time to come and see me perform. They even overlooked the newspaper coverage. But the play was a great success and was selected for the youth festival at Jaipur.

***

THE JOURNEY TO Jaipur was hot and uncomfortable. I felt claustrophobic in the dormitory which we were stuffed into, like sardines. I would go for early morning walks. The desert topography somehow made me lapse into the barrenness of life. It seemed that Age challenged Time and raced ahead, making us older each moment. What was this thing we called life? Did it dry up each day like a carcass?

Savita would often break into my reverie. "How do you like this place, Malvika?"

"It's different...quite pleasant...how do you like it?"

"I prefer Delhi. This town lives a dying history. The pink is so artificial. There are crowds...but only foreign tourists—it seems as if everything has been specially put up on display." Jivesh said, "It is so lonely here that I feel as if I've been banished from my country."

"I wonder how people stay here," said Mohan.

"Banished, Jivesh. You can feel dislodged within the walls of your own home. Sometimes a wandering mind is an experience in exile."

"Come, come, Malvika. Even you don't appear too happy here. You seem to be tired."

"Happiness can also be tiring and rapturous bliss can cause fatigue."

"And what, may I know, is the reason for your rapturous bliss?" Mohan said.

"Don't you understand? Sir is here—Bhupen Singh—the fountain of her rapturous bliss."

Jivesh laughed. I froze and Savita turned grey.

"No wonder our play has got a plain Jane as its heroine."

"Mohan, if you can't be respectful you can at least be civil," I felt hot tears of embarrassment tingling my eyes.

By evening a silence hung between Savita and me. I kept thinking about my attraction for Bhupen—it was so miniscule, so short-lived. What magical or magnifying lens had Mohan used to decipher it? I had not even given it a name—it was just there—a special flight in fantasy—belonging to me.

That evening was the dress rehearsal. We were all very self-conscious as if the hypocrisies of life had been turned into a performance. Savita made more than her share of mistakes. She would swallow the last words of her dialogue and the entire script would go haywire for lack of her cues.

"Savita, please emote clearly. You keep chewing your words," said Bhupen.

"Please Sir, don't be after me. I've told you, I'll perform perfectly on stage tomorrow." She made a face and walked away from the scene. I wasn't on stage. Savita came and sat next to me. I tried to console her.

"Stones would be left unhewn if it weren't for the chisel—surely you wouldn't grudge a chisel for sculpturing form into a stone?"

"I think you're out to enact Bhupen's ideas in real life." There was loud laughter. Just then Bhupen came up and his cold voice stated his attempt to control his annoyance.

"Savita, you should not have walked off in a huff. Come along, let's complete the scene."

"No Sir, I am not in the mood. I'll perform well tomorrow, I promise." Bhupen left the hall and we dispersed to our rooms.

The play went off well. I got the best performance award for the main role and Savita bagged it for her supporting role.

There was a poetic soiree in the evening. We sat amidst the audience and suddenly I heard Bhupen's name being announced for a rendering of a song by Rabindranath Tagore. I heard the group whispering, nudging each other and giggling—but I was enchanted by Bhupen's voice that reached out to the stars.

"I feel that all the stars shine in me. The world breaks into my life like a flood. The flowers blossom in my body. All the youthfulness of land and water smokes like an incense in my heart, and the breath of all things plays on my thoughts as if on a flute. When the world sleeps I come to your door. The stars are silent and I am afraid to sing. I wait and watch till your shadow passes by the balcony of night and I return with a full heart. Then in the morning I sing by the roadsides. The flowers in the hedge give me answers and the morning air listens."

***

IT WAS OUR last day in Jaipur, and we went to see the city that bore tales of chivalry, of people who had withstood the ravages of time and yet risen each time, buoyant from the pressure—making calamity a whetstone to courage. That was how James Tod, the famous historian, had written about the people of Rajasthan. We went around the city, surrounded by rugged hills and castles and we could feel the slumbering history. Jaipur had been founded by Maharaja Sawai Jaisingh who had applied the principles of the ancient Indian treatise *Shilpa Shastra* to build it.

On the eve of British Prince Albert's visit in 1875, Maharaja Ram Singh had the main bazaar of the City mantled pink. Since then, pink had become its characteristic colour, leading to the popular name Pink City.

The bazaars we passed through were arrayed with Sanganeri and tie and dye prints, enamelled brass work, marble stationery, precious jewellery, pottery, ivory and sandalwood artifacts and embroidered clothes and shoes.

We started from 'Chaura-Raasta', the main street to the Mubarak Mahal, which has now become a museum. It houses a private collection of the royal family. It contained a large and varied collections of costumes and jewellery belonging to the former rulers. Bhupen walked with me many times, participating with the guide and telling me so many things which the guide forgot to mention. We both stood on one of the curved arches of the window of Hawa Mahal or the Palace of Winds. I was very disappointed to see it. Hawa Mahal had only face and no depth. Bhupen explained to me: "Don't be disappointed Malvika, this is not a Palace but a sort of group of projecting balconies. From here, queens, princesses, courtesans, maids and slave girls looked down upon the forbidden world outside."

"Maybe they came here during some festival or maybe to watch the brave Rajput warriors marching for the battle."

"Have you noticed," Jeevesh said, "the architecture is so perfect that every little window is placed in such a manner that a constant current of air keeps the whole interior cool."

"No Jivesh, the princesses came here to look at their Prince Charmings and to start or end their romances with them." Savita's eyes were full of a mischievious expression when she said that.

I agreed that the Museum was loaded with an air of romance...everything was so beautiful—the collection of paintings, sculptures, jewels, stone-studded arms—all had an aroma of romance. There were fine illustrations of *Bhagavad Gita* on a grain of rice and a very rare *Gita Gobinda* of the 16th century with exquisite paintings. One could see the painters had used gold very lavishly on the paintings. Bhupen was fascinated with the arms—I was impressed with the enamel and inlay work and the artistic engravings of the jewels on the arms. Bhupen was asking a lot of questions. As he talked, one vein near his ear would swell up. Bhupen was definitely different from Jivesh or Mohan. I liked the animal like personality of Bhupen—to be an animal is to be very natural. Bhupen was most keen on the ancient armour and listened to the legends attached to them with great avidity. His demeanour of single minded concentration somehow had an attraction about it. His restrained decorum seemed to have a strange undertone of primeval masculinity. Suddenly I realised Bhupen was lost in the past, unfolding the folded past and I was lost in him.

As we came out, we came across a folk singer dressed up in typical Rajasthani attire. He was singing for our group. For him, everyday was an occasion of celebration. In India each season has songs. It was a haunting lyric. Our guide told us that these kind of singers are known as 'Langas' and that they were in great demand in the rural areas. They were the main entertainers even earlier and were continuing to be so even today.

He was singing 'Gorbandh'. 'Gorbandh' is a kind of

decoration which women used to make for the cattle of the house. Rajasthani handicraft is used even for decorating cattle or any other animal they use in their daily life.

"Precious Gorbandh
How bright
How intricate in pattern
Lovely to behold
How gracefully you adorn
My camel's neck."

I was thinking, India is the only nation in the world where animals are worshipped, specially the cow, which plays an important role in ones life. Horses, monkeys or even snakes—there are so many festivals with references in folk songs about animals.

***

ON REACHING DELHI, we were felicitated for our successful performance and Bhupen invited the entire cast for tea. There was something different about Bhupen. I felt all my perceptions reflected in him and a strange kinship was established between us. I generally picked up Savita on the way while on outings together. But I didn't find her at home that day. I went alone to Bhupen's house. He lived in one of the Staff quarters in the college campus. The door was wide open and I could see a beautifully kept room. There was nothing ostentatious about it; there was cane furniture and some books neatly stacked on the wall near a rocking chair. The plants in carved earthen pots had a simple rural appeal that was not vulgarly ethnic. I entered and stood gazing at the bookshelf which comprised of novels, books on philosophy and a number of biographies. What would anyone gain by reading biographies? I mused. What was it like to peep into other people's lives. Just then Bhupen entered the room with a tray laden with cups and saucers. He was a little taken aback to see me there.

"When did you arrive?"

"I've just come," I said, not meeting his eyes out of embarrassment.

"What are you doing with this tray?"

"Chottu hasn't turned up again today."

"Let me help you." I took the tray from his hands and started arranging the crockery on the table. "Do you read a lot?"

"Books are the only true companions of life."

"Do you mostly go for biographies? Don't the conclusions and inspirations of other peoples lives seem a little untrue and stale?"

"Oh no," he laughed. I felt the same vibrations of animal attraction in his laughter, wild but attractive. "I read biographies merely to understand why people react as they do, or maybe how I would react in a similar situation of life."

"I never imagined there were such nuances to a biography."

"Sometimes books arouse thinking to the point of restlessness."

"How is that?"

"Once while waiting for the red light to change at a crossing, I was pondering about something I had read and did not notice it changing to green till the traffic policemen appraised me of a minor traffic jam behind me."

"What were you thinking about?"

"I will have to think about that too...Oh yes.. I was thinking about Paul Gaugin abandoning his promising bank career and family to settle in Tahiti."

"As far as I know he had an unhappy married life and was quite unattached to his family."

"I suppose when the manifestation of art becomes larger than life, one rises above all the worldly attachments."

"I don't think anyone has the right to be indifferent to responsibility for the sake of his own selfish vision or love."

"But Malvika, love is blind…

"Whose love is blind?"

Jivesh asked in a dramatic tone as he entered. His jibe was obviously aimed at me. Savita was right behind with annoyance written plainly on her face. She looked all painted up with make-up applied dexterously probably at a beauty parlour—expensive but artificial.

"Hello Jivesh…Hi Savita…You're looking lovely. That's a beautiful saree you're wearing."

Savita's face assumed a softness hearing this. "Do you like it? Thank you."

I kept arranging the table. Bhupen handed me some of the snacks to be served. I wondered how he had managed to arrange all this by himself. Suddenly, I felt Savita by my side. She practically snatched the plates from me and started giving them out with a vengeance. She went about her work with the confidence of a housewife. I went back to the book rack. Khalil Gibran, Plato, Brecht, Sartre, Machiavelli—were there in all their glory. I felt the stirrings of desire in myself—but of what, I did not know. It was a desire—strange but sweet. There on the flyleaf of a book was written, "I wish for a never ending completeness."

I stopped short—why did Bhupen feel incomplete; what didn't he have? Knowledge…the ability to write so beautifully…an attractive personality...what did he find elusive...material wealth? Do material assets really fulfill all ones desires? Why then, who would be the most complete person? By completeness he meant a situation where you don't stand to lose anything. What had Bhupen lost? Could I make up for it? I felt the same strange inexplicable desire creeping up again. Why does desire arise just like that—without a valid reason or right to be there.

"Hey, what are you doing there, Malvika? You can read those books later…come and join us. Sir has consented to sing some Rabindra Sangeet." Jivesh pulled me back to the crowd.

Bhupen was on his rocking chair. Savita was on a low stool by his feet, offering him something out of her own plate.

"Please start your song, Sir. Malvika has come." Bhupen closed his eyes in concentration and sang, immersed in the feelings of the great poet Tagore.

"Life of my life, I shall ever try to keep my body pure, knowing that thy luring touch is upon all my limbs.

I shall ever try to keep all untruths out from my thoughts, knowing that thou art that truth which has kindled the light of reason in my mind.

I shall ever try to keep my body pure, knowing that thou art that truth which has kindled the light of reason in my mind. I shall ever try to drive all evils away from my heart and keep my love in flower knowing that thou hast thy seat in the inmost shrine of my heart.

And it shall be my endeavour to reveal thee in my actions, knowing it is thy power gives me strength to act.

I ask for a moment's indulgence to sit by thy side. The works I have in hand I will finish afterwards."

"What a resonant voice you have," said Savita. The pallu of her saree had slipped down. She had assumed a seductive posture that displayed her ample proportions. Bhupen unconsciously merged into the depths of the scene. The rest were busy chatting, eating and generally enjoying themselves. I was stunned. Was it by Savita's conquettish behaviour or the subtle connotations of the song Bhupen had sung—I did not know.

***

MY DESIRE ENTERED my consciousness as another of life's questions. If this desire of mine was love, was it something to be possessed? Did it exist between Papa and Mother who never tired of each other and only spoke in endearments—'Darling', 'Sweetheart', 'Love'. And the gossip about Grandfather, who had bequeathed a huge mansion in Mussoorie to a nautch girl whom he fell in love with? Was giving of property, another name for love? Some kind of a Taj Mahal sentiment? I reflected about my relationship with my parents—what did I desire of them—I could not say.

I would have to eliminate my inadequacies, in order to understand myself better. I wanted to look at life as an artist looks at his landscape.

I liked to be near Bhupen all the time. I liked the masculine aroma that he exuded. Being close to him had brought me closer to myself. I wanted to know him better and my mind would be in a turmoil just thinking about him. Was this love, then?

"Bitto—you didn't tell me it was your birthday." Bhaiji's voice brought me out of my reverie.

"My birthday—that's been over a long time now."

"You crazy child. Do you know better than your mother? She has told me that she's celebrating your birthday with a party and you say it's over."

"Mother is celebrating my birthday…but why? She never has. And what kind of a birthday is this? On an inappropriate day?"

"Don't you know—She's invited lots of people—how do you think I'm here?. We've ordered a big cake for you… all the arrangements for the party have been made…you'll remain a crazy child," Bhaiji admonished affectionately and went inside.

But my birthday had gone by stealthily without even a whisper, so what was this birthday party being organised for?

"Malvika, give your measurements for a dress to the tailor," Mother called impatiently.

"But why a dress?"

"For you…tomorrow is the party, you will need a new dress."

"But I never wear these kind of dresses."

"So what? There'll be so many important people coming—you must appear fashionable before them."

"No," I insisted, "I will not wear a dress. I am not going to meet any of your important people—in any case. I never attend any of your parties."

"The new Commissioner is here—so Papa thought of this ploy, to invite him over. We've told everyone it's your birthday."

I left the room. 'Ploy' was probably of more significance

than feelings—it could trample over them.

Mother appeared with four of her own sarees. "Okay, don't be angry, wear any of these…whichever one you like. The invitation cards have been sent out. You will have to attend this party."

I had not even seen the invitation cards. I kept the sarees without any further comment.

On the evening of the party the house was flooded with well-known personalities. There were hordes of gifts—an apology of a sentiment. My birthday had become a bargain offer and I did not figure in it anywhere. Mother's hollow laughter was surrounded by the plastic people in their synthetic apparel with pallid glassy faces made to look bright, with colours. I cut the birthday cake with my name on it. "Happy Birthday to you," resounded with a senseless childishness.

I escaped to the precincts of the lawn. It was cool and green and gave off a soothing quietude. The fuming orange sun had no option but to set into the horizon. My love for the sun was reiterated each morning when I arose. I saw the sun rise out of the sky spreading a new day of life, filling me with hope. But the setting sun always gave me a sinking deep inside.

"Hey, what are you doing here?" Bhupen…here, in my lawn? I should have been asking that question.

"I came to pick up my Uncle, the Commissioner, and

when I reached here I realised this is your house and today is your birthday. But I couldn't see you or any of your friends."

"It's not my birthday. It's the ghost of a day long dead."

"Please don't say that. The day you were born is not in the past—it's the present…today…with you…a truth of your existence."

"If you wish to turn an ugly falsehood into the truth, then…"Would it never leave me—the stirrings of my desire—like a turbulent storm, blowing all reason away. I trembled, not knowing how or when it happened. Under the lengthening shadows of the tree his lips were on mine. His whispers filled me with…what was it…joy, a throbbing pain, restlessness or only the hint of my desire—leaving me in a trance.

Bhupen was looking at me with a smile on his lips and a tune under his breath. I stood against the trunk of the tree, trying to gather my wits about me. The darkness was pierced by the silver light of the moon—a full moon, which could rage a fever in the tides of the sea.

***

THE BODY SPEAKS its own language, with a diction more distinct than words—infusing life into living and making it more worthwhile.

Had it been Mother or Papa who loved to throw parties? There was another one being organised—cards were being sent out and telephonic invitations extended—it was a farewell to another year. A new year was to be born and people, as always, were anxious to trap and hold that moment in a tightly clenched grasp before it burst into a new life. The thought was titillating and I decided to attend the New Year Eve's celebration, to experience that moment of transition.

The house was filled with the smell of good cooking. The hall had been adequately decorated with ribbons and flowers. The music system with gigantic speakers waited patiently, anticipating the dancing that would soon fill the room. I wondered what kind of music would sweep me on to the dance floor. The telephone rang and Mother received the call.

"What—what are you saying?"

She slumped into a sofa. I rushed to retrieve the telephone from her hands but the line had got disconnected. "What is the matter Mother? Who was on the line? Please answer." My voice echoed in the empty room.

"Help...please help," I called out to no one in particular. The governess came running in. Just then I heard the painful screech of an ambulance.

"What's all this...Mother...Mother." But she lay there unconscious.

They took out a strange bundle wrapped in a white sheet and the doctor stepped forward.

"Are you Miss Nanda?"

"Yes...Yes...What's all this?"

"I am sorry, your father met with a terrible accident. He died on the spot."

The blood splattered bundle was Papa. Looking at it—the sluice gates burst open—Mother and I could not hold ourselves any longer.

I don't know how many days passed. Bhaiji, Mother and I would sit, staring at each other through the void. The prayers and rituals filled up our silence. On the traditional thirteenth day ceremony, the number of people among Papa's countless 'friends' who showed up were enough to make Mother cry helplessly. Amongst my friends only Jivesh and Mohan put in an appearance. I felt uneasy about Bhupen and Savita's absence. I heard Uncle's voice, a little sharp, breaking into my thoughtlessness.

"Please follow the rituals more carefully Malvika; pour the ghee into the sacred fire only when I say, *Swaha*—not before or after."

The priest started delivering his sermon. He recounted a tale from the *Mahabharat*. The five Pandava brothers wandered about the forest during their exile. Once, in search of water, they discovered a clear lake amidst the shrubbery. On approaching the lake, the youngest, Nakula, heard the voice of the God Yaksh forbidding him to drink the water till he was able to answer the five questions that would be put to him. In the event of his inability to answer them, he would be turned to stone. One by one the brothers Nakula,

Sahdeva, Bhima and Arjuna were turned to stone. Soon it was the eldest, Yuddhisthira's turn. He answered all the questions one by one. The last was "what is the inevitable truth of life that we prefer to forget?"

"Death," said Yuddhisthira, "is the unflinching truth of our life, which we know but like to forget." The Yaksh was happy at his appropriate answer and put back life into all the brothers.

True, we are all so busy grappling with life that we often forget that we have to go one day. Papa had organised the new year show for living it up. From whence had Death come with its clammy hands and snatched him away? Mother was still in a state of shock. Words of consolation failed to penetrate the cool exterior. Jivesh and Mohan leaned forward towards me.

"Very sorry Malvika. We were shocked to hear about it. May God give you the courage to bear this loss."

"Savita didn't come," I couldn't resist asking.

"Actually," he hesitated, "She's getting married. She and Bhupen Sir, that's why they couldn't come. I hope you'll excuse us, Malvika. We are going to have to attend the wedding."

They left—as did all the other guests. I don't know how long Mother and I lay silently in our rooms. Mother had become lifeless amidst such a sudden tragedy—I was unable to steady her. My seventeen years seemed too young and weak to provide her courage. Mother was thirty-five. I was mature enough to understand and she was young enough to be understood. I understood her. I wanted to console her, but I had no healing touch, neither education nor any economic support.

I had let Bhupen into the recesses of my heart. What was it that had made him marry Savita? Try as I did, I could not understand or justify this. Why? But, there were more crucial questions and more urgent ones to be tackled. The house we occupied was official, and would have to be vacated at once.

***

THE SERIES OF walls that had hitherto enfolded us to form a home had to be bid farewell. We got into the waiting car. Mother cried unashamedly that day. Her demeanour ravaged with the vagaries of widowhood did not seem her own. It was not difficult to imagine the enormity of thought processes that flowed through her mind. The stress of leaving home and all its trappings of security undoubtedly contributed to her anguish. Uncle sat in the front seat of the car. He strained to look at her every few minutes, and wiped the unshed tears from the corner of his eyes.

"I had accompanied brother to bring you home as a new bride. You had looked so young and radiant and we were all so happy. Had we ever imagined that he would leave us all so soon. He was more a son than a brother to me. What test of Time is this? Dear God...look after these two souls...

they are innocent in the ways of the world."

Mother could not stop the fresh flow of tears. I was very quiet—lost in the events of the incomplete dream I had been rudely woken from. I felt no remorse at leaving that house. I had no attachments with it except Papa, who did not stay there anymore. I felt the loss of the past—a rising desire that had been smothered by the brute force of mishap. Mother and I shared the same affliction—though the reasons that had brought it on were quite different. Waves of agitated thoughts surged in the mind. Uncle dozed off and drowsily groaned…"Oh God…Dear Lord," as if in pain.

We stopped for snacks at a wayside dhaba and by evening we had reached Mussoorie. We passed the Library area and the steep climb in front of the Savoy. The winding roads were empty and devoid of any people. The sudden change in topography and weather was exhausting. But we would have to familiarise ourselves with these roads. We would soon be walking them—whether strange, lonely, steep or winding.

"Here we are, 'Nirmal-Kunj' for you, Abha." Bhaiji turned towards me, "Bitto—Please organise the luggage."

Bhaiji got off the car. The watchman saluted him and hastened to open the huge gate.

The Haveli looked magnificent, with an aroma of the past whispering its secrets. It was a white stone construction typical of British architecture. It looked old and grey but had a quiet strength about it and was not dilapidated in any way. It stood solidly carved in limestone, with four Gothic pillars on its portals. A series of circular stone steps led up to the front verandah and into the unknown future. We started ascending the steps when all at once a young man clutching some books brushed past us and raced down the stairs. The books fell from his hands at the landing. He hastily picked them up and fled from the house.

"Who is that? Stop, who is that? How did he get in?" Bhaiji called out.

"I don't know his name, Sir. He comes to meet Janaki sometimes. He borrows books from her."

"Who is Janaki, Bhaiji," I asked.

"She is the housemaid. Her father used to be the chief caretaker. Janaki was born and brought up here. She stayed on after her marriage. Her husband also works here at Nirmal Kunj."

We entered the hall. It was quite bare but for a couple of pictures which hung on the walls and some old pieces of furniture covered with white drapes. The room was full of secrets, waiting to be unearthed.

"Namaskar, Sarkar." She had suddenly appeared from nowhere. Dark of complexion but with sculpturesque features, she was short-statured yet extremely attractive. Her white saree, fresh and worn with care, was impressive.

"How are you Janaki?"

"I am fine, Sarkar. Is this the choti bahu?"

'Yes this is Bahu Rani…Abha…and this is her daughter Malvika…Bitto…"

"Oh, her daughter. I thought she was her sister." She giggled and her white teeth flashed from her dusky face and the sweet bitter smell of betel leaf and tobacco filled the musty room. "Bitto's face looks so familiar…I thought Baijee…Didiji you've come for the first time to Nirmal Kunj. Not once in all these years did you ask after our welfare."

"Janaki, why did you say my face looks familiar?" I asked.

"No particular reason, Didiji."

"Come along," said Uncle briskly, "Bring us some tea. Abha is very tired. She's been crying the whole way."

"It's been an enormous calamity, Sir, such a young age and…"

"Where are the washrooms Janaki? Mother why don't you have a wash and freshen up?" I tried to change the topic, fearing Mother's reaction at Janaki's extended sympathy.

Mother proceeded inside and Uncle pulled up a chair and sat in the verandah, He started talking in soft tones to Bedi, the butler he had brought with him. Janaki took me on a conducted tour of Nirmal Kunj. The central round hall had a wooden dance floor and a dais at one end, obviously meant for a live band. The carved furniture was antique with velvet cushions that had not faded with time. Portraits lined the walls and the spaces between them with empty nailheads denoted the pictures that had once been there. "Maria—1722" was written on the panel of one…a princess from the lost pages of history or may be the artist's beloved, I conjectured.

Venetian glass covered an entire wall. It had engraved flowers with colours so fresh, they seemed dripped in dew. Mother had come into the room. There was no reaction at the decayed opulence. She looked at the empty protruding nails.

"Where have these pictures gone, Janaki?"

"They have been removed—they belonged to Baijee. This had always been a room of special significance to her. What a lovely person she was—she wasn't good looking at all, but somehow she appeared very graceful. She had qualities beyond compare. She used to throw parties with varied ambiences. She would be completely at ease with the English memsahibs who used to visit us. She danced with their music and spoke their language. And when there were Urdu poets with their romantic couplets she would speak in chaste Urdu and wear the traditional Muslim dress—the long flowing 'garara', and 'Kamdani Kurta'. Grandfather was very fond of singing 'Kajri' when it rained. Then she would sit by him wearing a brocade skirt—a ghagra draped with a tie and dye 'Odhni'. She was certainly not a nautch girl as people called her. She simply loved grandfather and had given up everything to live with him, for him. She even wore the jewellery considered auspicious for a married woman—she really doted on your Grandfather."

"Was she a Hindu or a Muslim?"

"I only know she was a Kashmiri."

"Then she must have been pretty."

"No, not at all, inspite of being a Kashmiri. In fact she looked a lot like you Bitto Didi."

"Me?" I laughed.

"What rubbish are you talking?" We heard Bhaiji's voice booming.

"Honestly Sarkar, you had never seen her. But I literally played in her lap as a child."

"Where is she now?" Mother asked.

"No one knows. She just vanished after Grandfather's death. None of us knew when she left."

"Surely there must be a picture or some belonging of hers in this house?"

"How can there be? These people have lived off the knick knacks of this house," Bedi said.

"How dare you accuse us. I have always looked after this Haveli. I haven't even left it to go to my in-law's home, after I got married."

'You would have if you had one. Your husband also stays here, eating off his wife's earnings," Bedi laughed.

"Damn you...."

"Please stop this nonsense," Uncle intervened. "Bitto, come and see your room."

Janaki escorted Mother to what had been Joharbai's bedroom. There was a plain four poster bed but a rather elaborate dressing table, fabulous and sparkling with a past glory. Besides this room there were six bedrooms on the top floor and four on this one. They were all practically empty. I selected a corner room for myself. Mother wanted me to share her room but I was used to a separate one for myself. Mother and I were poles apart. She would be getting up late in the mornings—a habit she had inculcated as the idle spoilt wife. I was used to reading late at night and rising early. I planned to do up my room according to my taste. I got the huge carved double bed cut into a single one and converted the rest of the wood into a study table and a book rack. There were plenty of books in the house.

Some of them had a name written in Urdu on the flyleaf and some had simply 'J' written on them. Almost all the books were on music, art or Indian philosophy and culture or on well known places of India. They were all rare masterpieces to be preserved. Joharbai had apparently been fluent in English and Urdu. My room was soon full of books. I shifted my bed to the balcony that had been fully covered with glass and latticed stone. Mother was annoyed to see the arrangements in my room. 'Why did you have to cut up such a beautiful bed to make a silly book rack. It was such an expensive piece."

My comfort to me was a part of my discipline and wealth. I rememberd what Bhupen had once said, "Discipline brings with it refinement, moral courage and peace of mind. It is discipline that strengthens the body and provides us with the necessary freedom we desire in life."

"Have you managed to reach this threshold of discipline that opens out into these benefits?"

"I don't know Malvika. But I do make an attempt." Was his liaison with Savita a part of this attempt? I shouldn't be thinking of all this. I had to make a new start in life. But I was standing at a dead end? I had to muster the strength for the initial step...I had never really known Bhupen and yet had made substantial investments of my happiness in him. The one person in this world on whom I had pinned all my hopes and beliefs. I had not wanted to know him better, lest I be disillusioned. I did not want to redesign the perfect man I had once imagined. I certainly did not fancy picking up my pencil again to sketch another outline. The steadfastness of character and graciousness of personality that I had sought, was still a part of my perspective of Bhupen. I wished to retain it as an integral part of myself. The existence of Savita in all this did not bother me. There was no place for sorrow, jealousy or hatred. I really cared for Bhupen—that was all that mattered. Love in reality was quite different from what was often enacted on stage.

***

BHAIJI LEFT US to fend for ourselves at Nirmal Kunj. We felt isolated in these new and harsh roles. Mother and I would spend the greater part of the day in our rooms, doing nothing. Mother had become quite lifeless while I tried to regain my grasp on life. The business of resettling in Nirmal Kunj had an unaesthetic effect. There is little scope for wallowing in sorrow, amidst diligence.

Bedi helped us out in all this, while Janaki tried to reconstruct the fragmented history of the house for our amusement. She told us that Grandfather belonged to a big Zamindar family of his time. They owned seven villages around Dehradun. Grandfather was sent to England to study Law. He was not only an attractive personage but a cultured one. On his return from England, people from far and near would come to see him, as if he was no longer human but had developed into an image worthy of homage. They would be in awe of his handsome bearing.

During this period, the Zamindar of Chattari sent the marriage proposal of his daughter for Grandfather. The messenger who carried the tidings of the proposal was weighed in seven kinds of grain which were distributed among the poor; and he was sent back happily loaded with gifts in gold and silver. The people of the village rejoiced and prayed for the bridegroom to be, who soon left the illuminated, gaily decorated homestead for the bride's house with an adequately represented marriage party. They were entertained with lavish feasts and exotic dancing girls for five days. The bride's people spared no effort in their hospitality. But ironically, the nubile girl bedecked in all her bridal finery remained firmly entrenched behind the heavy curtains of the Palanquin, while Joharbai with her melodious voice and enchanting eyes captivated the heart of my Grandfather, Lala Govardhan.

Saryu Devi, now Lala Govardhan's lawfully wedded wife placed her elegantly hennaed feet on the threshold of the Dehradun homestead amidst pious chantings and rituals befitting a newly wedded bride; while in the congested part of the city Joharbai took up cheap lodgings in a back lane. Lala Govardhan entrusted the family honour to his bride, and proceeded to extricate himself from the heavy shackles of peerage to get submerged in the joys of loving and living with Joharbai. The innocent bride became completely isolated amidst the quiet of the huge mansion that did not resound with any excitement or childish prattle. The silence deepened each day, while Joharbai's flat came alive with the twinkling of dancing feet and reverberated with the sonorous notes of classical and traditional music. Nirmal Kunj was soon built at Mussoorie to alleviate the long humid days of the summer.

Many years passed and Lala Govardhan's business prospered in proportion to the descending gloom in his house. Suddenly there was a whispering among the women of the family. Saryu Devi was expecting a child in her middle age. Bhaiji's birth was not only a joyous occasion but a turning point in the life of Saryu Devi. Lala Govardhan unceremoniously sent back the maid who brought the news of the happy event and refused to set his eyes on the newborn.

Saryu Devi's mother who had come from Chattari, sensed what was amiss. She started counselling her daughter on the clever intricacies of a successful wife. She took on Grandfather's indifference as a challenge and would often leave the newborn freshly wrapped in soft velvet in his room. Succumbing to its cries one day, he picked up the infant.

It was as if fate had finally decided to shower Saryu Devi with the long denied happiness. The flicker of a tiny lamp is enough to dispel the darkness. The little one became the cynosure of Grandfather's eyes and Grandmother's aged countenance finally shone with the joys of marital bliss.

Papa was bom seven years later. Both the boys were at school when they lost their father. After Grandpa's demise, Grandma took over the task of running the household and looking after her children with complete dedication. Along with their studies she made sure they were well versed in the scriptures. A Panditji was called in each Sunday to teach them the subtleties of religious ceremonies like havan mantras and other rituals. Grandfather had not left them much to subsist on. Much of his wealth had been squandered on the extravagances of debauched living. The end had come before he could be seriously concerned about the children's future.

Grandmother managed her life adequately. Bhaiji shared

much of the onus of her responsibility. He undertook never to marry probably as a reaction to his father's lifestyle. Papa got through the Indian Civil Services and got absorbed in his career. Grandmother got him married early. Mother was sixteen when she was married to Papa. Grandmother died the next year—the year I was born. Mother and Papa were always out on postings and hardly ever stayed at Dehradun. And, now of course, circumstances had brought her permanently to Mussoorie. No one knew how Bhaiji had managed to retrieve Nirmal Kunj or what had happened to Joharbai.

Bhaiji would always visit us, his car loaded with sacks of wheat, rice and tins of cooking medium. He came to advise us and to see for himself how independent we had become. I was never reminded of Papa when I saw him. I could feel the burns of his raging sorrow and my mind would throb with the restless hammering of his despair. His words of consolation evoked no response in us—they were more appropriate for himself.

***

THE SERVANTS ASSISTED us in converting Nirmal Kunj into a small hotel. The external verandah had become the reception area. Five dining sets had been arranged in the dining hall. The round hall with its dance floor had become the lobby. Mother became busy, if not happily occupied. There were brief moments of discovery between us. Mother and I began to understand each other. It was like the realisation between two strangers—more incidental than by choice. Mother would suddenly appear with a saree in my room. "Malvika, why don't you try on this saree—this colour is too bright for me to wear."

And after a moment, "Oh I did not realise...you wear Salwar Kameez more often...but aren't you old enough now... you'll be nineteen this birthday."

"No mother," I said quietly, "I will be twenty two."

"Oh I see," she looked flustered and left.

Later that evening, at dinner, she looked intently at me and said, "I'm so crazy—I hadn't thought of your settling down. Next time Bhaiji is here I will tell him to look for a suitable match for you."

"Don't worry Mother, I don't wish to get married."

"Why not? You're just at the right age. I was barely sixteen when I married your Papa and eleven months later you were born."

"Those were different times Mother," I blurted out, knowing I had put forth a weak argument.

"But you'll have to get married Malvika. I wonder why it never struck your father."

"I wasn't so old then mother. Besides, I was at college."

"But you're still studying, you should have finished college by now." She seemed to be mentally calculating.

"Mother, I've completed my postgraduation. I'm writing my thesis for my doctorate and am teaching at the Convent school."

"You're working? Since when and why? You never asked me."

"I've got accustomed to choosing my own paths in life Mother."

She kept staring at me blankly. Perhaps it had finally dawned on her that I never asked her for any money. Perhaps she had realised that the kitchen always ran, even in the absence of tourists.

Once she came up with a suggestion, "Malvika your hair has grown so long. Why don't you have it cut. Your Papa always thought that short hair looked so much smarter."

She lapsed into memory lane and then said, "Malvika do you think I should grow my hair? After all I'm a widow—what do you think people will say?"

"How does it matter what people say? Short hair suits you. Please be as you are...smart."

At dinner she would suddenly stop eating, and stare at the table set with cheap crockery. "Why did he have to provide for me so well? I'm repaying for all the luxuries I had got used to."

I went around the table to comfort her. She looked up at me and said, "Malvika did you find the food exotic or tasty? I cannot recollect when and what you ate. Your governess used to take care of all that. In any case, we were seldom home for dinner."

She would lapse thus into the past—sometimes she would leave the table abruptly to give vent to her tears. All the happy events of the past had been transformed into painful memories and weaknesses of the present. I couldn't remember there ever being a relationship between my palate and the exercise of eating. I was quite used to gulping down whatever food my governess served me. My taste buds had probably never developed the capacity to distinguish one food from another. I was the happier for it, I thought wryly.

I tried to counsel Mother. "The taste of food lies within yourself, not in these curries. After all, we eat only as an obligation towards our body—to keep it going. Hapiness is all in the mind. It may stem from the external gratification of any one of the senses—but contentment can only come from within."

"Where have you learnt to talk so well, dear? Have you learnt it from Bhaiji?"

I laughed out, aloud. We decided that we would get the dining hall waiter to serve us and dispense with Bedi. We would eat at one of the tables in the dining hall but there was generally nothing ready in the hotel kitchen. The few tourists who came, booked for lodging only minus the meals. This had been the primary cause of my having to take up a job. The revenue from the hotel was not enough to run the house.

***

MY TEACHING ASSIGNMENT at the convent was accompanied with obligatory clerical work, which the ill-natured Principal, Sister Martha, had thrust upon me. It was only then that she condescended to disburse the meagre twenty thousand rupees that had been fixed as my salary. I would often think of leaving the school when I tired of Sister Martha's insufferable bearing but the compulsion of running the house and the uncertain state of my academic achievements held me back. I had yet to complete my studies. I tried to discipline my mind to adapt itself to the environment of the convent. My spirit rebelled and there was no path to freedom. The handful of tourists that drifted into Nirmal Kunj would soon vanish, once the 'Season' was over.

Several slopes had been terraced and levelled to create Mussoorie, which now had nothing of the hills left in its character. The innumerable shops and hotels had only contributed to the devastation of its landscape and the pollution of the air around it. The whole place was like one big fair with crowds that left no space on its streets. The commencement of the tourist season brought on the shortage of all essentials—milk, bread, vegetables and even water. But like the other inhabitants, we still waited for the tourists from one season to the next.

The Convent lay well concealed in the folds of the hills that overlooked the city. Its colossal structure was designed on grand Gothic lines. The environment inside was incredibly British even after 40 years of independence from colonialism.

Most of the teachers were nuns—Indians in foreign apparel. The mix seemed somehow unauthentic and therefore unappealing. There was a constant current of stress in the atmosphere that was more disheartening than tiring. I often wondered when Indians would learn to be themselves? When would we stop trying to speak our native tongue with an alien accent? When would we unshackle ourselves from this peculiar complex of inferiority that had been thrust upon us by the Britishers? I could perceive no ray of hope in the prevailing gloom.

The children were the other remarkable feature of the school. Most of them came from broken homes…homes with single parents or parents staying abroad. They had few visitors and there was an obvious split to their personality. They were either temperamental and quarrelsome or withdrawn and obstinate. Sometimes, merely teaching them was a strain and establishing a rapport or friendliness, a feat. I was particularly moved by Mandira, a student of the sixth class. There was something in her enormous eyes that made one pause and think. She was an exceptionally quiet child, lost in an inexplicable silence. She would always invert and write the letter 'P', a habit she could not give up, even when reminded. We are initially accosted by impermeable rocks when drilling for water. I had reached the rocky layer and was quite sure my hands would one day be able to touch and mould the wet clay that lay beyond.

The solitude of Nirmal Kunj was really quite peaceful. It was on a hillside but the gardens that surrounded it created an illusion of plain ground. The lush front lawns were edged with different hued flower beds. A stately fountain in the shape of a mermaid carved in Italian marble adorned the centre.

The water gushed upwards from the lotus held in the mermaid's hands and poured in streamlets over her very shapely body. There were shady trees all around—flowering ones in front and many kinds of fruit at the back of the mansion. Whatever were Janaki's lapses, she had spared no effort to landscape the gardens with flowers and fruits. She would illustriously pluck the season's fruit, ripen them in huge baskets and then scurry with them to the market. She would spend the better part of the day and evening in the garden from where one could hear the strains of her lilting voice. She would sing songs befitting the season. During 'Phagun' (around mid March), she would sing 'Phag' and 'Hori'—songs customarily sung during Holi—the festival celebrated with the throwing of colours.

***

JANAKI'S SONGS HAD the effervescence of youth linked to life's beautiful fleeting moments. They were refreshing and free like a cool breeze. They had no room for any constraints, let alone sorrow, loneliness or want. Her ability to stay happy had helped her spend such long years all alone in the precincts of the massive construction that was Nirmal Kunj. I never saw her sad, pensive or lethargic. She always had something to do, singing all the while she worked. She even had her own perception of life, which she would inadvertently make known. Once, while cooking eggs, she observed the paradoxes the British had left us Indians with, right down to the frying pan. Most of us no longer ate a traditional breakfast of puris or parathas but had developed alien tastes for bread and eggs. Mother would be annoyed to hear her talk and I would ponder over her remarks that conveyed so much of the modern Indian psyche.

No one knew how old Janaki was, or the reasons why she did not have any children. But the occurrences in her room gave some inkling. Bedi called me one day, "Didi, there's an infernal commotion going on in Janaki's room—some chap is nearly killing her. I have tried to propitiate him but he refuses to listen."

Mother said, "So, what can Didi do about it? Try and pacify them yourself. These low caste people are bound to fight."

"Come along Bedi, I will see to the problem." I turned without waiting for any kind of reaction from mother.

That was the first time I was going towards Janaki's room. Her room was actually an entire annexe. Two rooms, a kitchen, washroom, verandah and terrace—it was a complete unit,

The door of one of the rooms was ajar and I could spy Janaki squatting on the floor crying plaintively. On reaching closer, I saw a dark complexioned middle-aged man reclining on a cot complacently puffing at his bidi. He quickly stood up when he saw me. Janaki was also startled out of her sobs and quietened down. "What happened Janaki? Who is this man—why were you both fighting?"

"He's my husband," she spoke a bit sharply, on the defensive. He has returned home after many days and says he will stay here now, and bring that bitch with him. How can a single sheath hold two swords...tell me didi."

'You're right, Janaki, no one else can take your place here." I turned towards the rough looking man. "How dare you talk of bringing another woman into the home of your wedded wife?"

"I really don't want to.But believe me madam, this Haveli is filled with love songs of Johar Bai and is charged with sex and shadows of her affair with your Dadaji. It is really intoxicating, the atmosphere. I am surprised you are not affected by it." His shameless gaze disturbed me more than his loud voice.

"Bedi, please throw this man out." His presence in the room spread a most unpleasant stench, reeking of disease. His crude voice, crass manner and stance—and even his face—were unbearably obnoxious. He displayed an uncouth one-upmanship and his eyes spoke of a cunning lecherousness. I felt my cheeks go hot with anger, "Get out of here—you stupid man. You have the tenacity to beat your wife when you yourself are at fault."

"Look who's talking. You people had thrown your Grandfather out of his own house—and your grandmother—the less said the better." He forced a mock laugh, "She's my wife…I can do what I want with her."

"I think you'd better go, Didi," Janaki intervened. "He is shameless. He's shown his face after two years. It's alright. I'll bear the brunt of his torments—it's my responsibility as a good wife."

I left in a huff. I had expected better from Janaki. I had thought she had the courage to live life the way she understood it—I had never expected to see her so weak.

"Have your bones broken then; we only came to rescue you," Bedi grumbled as he accompanied me.

"He is a man and possesses manly qualities, so he hits me," Janaki's high pitched voice had the same old pride to it.

"There's passion in the air of this house…passion…that envelops whoever…." I didn't wait to hear the rest of the taunts he spat out. I could not help realising the bitter truth behind Kishen Lal's words. After all, the mansion had been Grandfather's special chamber of debauchery—the scene of his excesses and lapses—I could imagine all that had gone on here during his time.

***

THE MECHANICAL RHYTHM of the steel almirah being opened and shut in Mother's room could be clearly heard from where I stood on the terrace. I could see the end of the road near Camel Back, winding its way via the skating rink to the noisy market place at Kurli. The cemetery was also clearly visible. On one of the graves was a devotedly carved statue of Lord Jesus. Perhaps, it was someone else's image that had been immortalised in stone—I had never really examined it closely. Maybe I imagined it was that of the Lord only because it stood in a graveyard. I had once read somewhere, "We all have a part of Christ in ourselves. When we are no longer alive, Christ continues to enliven our image." Maybe the image of the dead man was still alive in that statue..

There was a sudden downpour where my eyes had wandered. Nirmal Kunj and Camel Back remained dry. Why is the rain so selfish? Why does it pour so erratically leaving some places in floods and others so dry that one pines for each single drop. It stopped just as suddenly, and the sun reflected in the wet ground appeared quite feeble. Sometime in my childhood I had heard that sun and rain together meant a fox's wedding in the animal world. Whatever else comes to pass, a rainbow certainly breaks through each time.

From the adjacent room, I could hear the counting of linen in Janaki's voice which sounded quite off-key. She should have been singing in this glorious weather—instead she was indulging in polite conversation with Mother about the number of vacant and occupied rooms. This was the invariable routine—the tourists would arrive and leave—the linen of the rooms would be sorted, counted, washed and spread out again. There would be a welcome at one door and a farewell at the other. One had to change facial expressions with the quick precision of a juggler. I found it difficult to keep my face ready with the appropriate expression on it. Mother had quite a natural talent to handle such situations. I was generally at school on the occasions of these warm receptions and send-offs.

Sometimes I would deliberately steal away to Sharatji's house for the preparation of my thesis. Sharatji lived alone and everything in his house was improper. There is definitely a certain pathos in a man who has not arrived at a proper relationship with women and who has led a warped moral life like Oscar Wilde, who exclaimed, "Man cannot live with a woman, nor can he live without her." It is a very strange thing that no man has lived with a woman, inspite of the fact that from birth to death he is surrounded by women—his mother, wife, and daughters or even if he does not marry, he has still to depend on his sister like William Wordsworth, or depend on his house-keeper, like Herbert Spencer. No fine philosophy is going to save his soul if he cannot establish a proper relationship with his mother or sister or may be with his housekeeper. I remember Janaki also told me one story from our Indian mythology.

The story was like this. About four thousand years ago,

Lord Brahma (God of creation) took the beauty of the flowers, the songs of the birds, the colours of the rainbow, the kiss of the breeze, the laughter of the waves, the gentleness of the lamb, the cunning of the fox, the way-wardness of the clouds and the frankness of the shower and wove them into a female 'Pratham-Stree'. This female was presented to the man as his wife. The Hindu Adam known as 'Pratham-Purush' was happy to find a companion. They enjoyed life and the beauty of the world together. After a few days, 'Pratham-Purush' went to Lord Brahma and said, "Take this woman away from me, I cannot live with her." Brahma listened to his request and took the 'Pratham-Stree' away. But as the time passed, 'Pratham-Purush' felt lonely and again came to Brahma and requested, "Give me back my woman." He was given back his woman, but again after a few days he felt he could not live with her, and returned her to God.

The whole process was repeated three times. When finally 'Pratham-Purush' came the fourth time and complained that he could not live without his female companion, Brahmaji made him promise that he would not change his mind again and that he would throw in his lot with her, for better or worse, and they would live together on this earth as best they knew how. I do not think the picture has essentiality changed much from 'Pratham-Purush' to the modern man of today.

I wondered how Janaki knew so much? This was such a meaningful story. Suddenly, I thought of Janaki. She was supposed to get me tea and sandwiches. I was about to shout her name and there she was with the tray.

"Didiji eat fast, Memsahib has just got up from her afternoon nap, she will be furious if she comes to know about the food being served in the bedroom."

"Don't worry." I started eating. I was very tired and hungry after all the work Sharatji made me do.

"Janaki, tell me how much have you studied and from where you heard that story of Pratham-Purush?"

"Joharbai ji was my teacher, Didiji. She used to narrate all these stories. She was very knowledgeable and she was the one who used to sing all the songs I sing. Her voice was like a koyal's. I cannot compete with her, but of course that is how I remember her."

"Didiji, someone has come to see you." I sprang out of my reverie.

"Who is it, Bedi?" I asked.

"A lady."

I stepped into the reception where an extremely attractive woman in a pair of black jeans and a shocking pink sweater sat perfectly composed on the sofa. She sported colourful strings and bangles that offset her thick black and closely cropped hair. Her dusky complexion and large eyes accentuated the sharpness of her features and added to her strong sex appeal. I recalled at once—she was something of a minor celebrity—a famous model and dancer. She had visited the school a couple of times but I had never spoken to her. She was never there on the Parent Teacher Day and would invariably arrive at the busiest hour during the school day. And now, she was here at my house, at an odd hour in the evening. She neither wished me nor offered her hand to greet me, and yet, I did not feel the need for any introductions between us.

'You're Mandira's..." I was hesitant to call her the mother of a twelve-year-old girl.

'Yes, I'm Mandira's mother, Nayantara, but you can call me Naina." A look of comraderie spread over her face as she spoke.

"I'm Mandira's class teacher."

"Yes, I know—Mandira keeps talking of you."

I took her to my room. I don't know how long we kept talking. Bedi replenished our teacups several times. It seemed I wanted to unravel all the knots closeted within me. My silences had found an outlet to gush out noisily. Naina too apparently wanted to bare her soul. She was an exponent of Bharat Natyam and Kuchipudi.

I recollected having read an article on her in one of those society magazines—her marriage to an affluent businessman, their incompatibility and subsequent divorce.

"I want to conduct Bharat Natyam classes. I'll have to occupy myself somehow, if I have to stay here. I think I should provide Mandira with the security of a home—an incomplete one—but a home nevertheless. I think all of us have a right to rise above the circumstances life places us in."

"Yes of course. We can go and speak to the Principal—or if you can take a room here at Nirmal Kunj and open a school," I said, taking an instant decision.

"Thanks...that's very kind of you, but I think the environment of the school would be more appropriate. The children won't have a problem attending the classes. Those who wish to, can stay back after school."

"Okay, I'll talk with the Principal. Can you reach school by noon tomorrow? We can have lunch together."

"Dinner is ready," Bedi's voice broke into our eager plans.

"What's the time?" We glanced at the clock.

"Good heavens. It's eight-thirty. I should be leaving now. I'll see you at school tomorrow Malvika."

"How can you leave without dinning Madam? You are the only one to have visited Didiji in all these years."

"Yes Naina, please stay for dinner. Bedi will escort you back later."

Naina agreed and I introduced her to Mother at the dining table. Janaki unobstrusively laid an extra plate and Naina took her place at the table as if she were accustomed to dining here every day. I could sense Mother taking in Naina's natural sophistication and recoiling at the simple food and ordinary crockery. She soon let down her defences on observing her informal bearing. Naina had done away with the cheap cutlery meticulously laid by the plate and was eating her meal with her fingers.

"You can use a fork, Naina. Bedi, you haven't laid the table properly."

Naina spoke unhurriedly "Its alright aunty. I don't believe in aping an alien culture. If we are aware of ourselves and our origins—why not be proud of them? I like to eat with my fingers, be Indian."

I could see Mother's fork slipping from her fingers at Naina's spirited reaction to her suggestion.

"Don't you think so aunty?" Naina carried on with her point of view. "Human beings are most imitative in their approach. If you've ever watched a man shaving—you'll see him making a thousand grimaces like a monkey. Whoever designed the motor car, based it on the human face. The front bonnet looks like two big jaws and the headlights appear to be eyes. There's really nothing new under the sun. It's all an imitation of something that already exists. Even the mechanics of the car is fashioned on the power man feels within himself. So he lets this machine loose on the roads—to run indiscriminately and crush everything that comes under its wheels."

"You're very interesting...what did you say your name was...yes, Nayantara."

"Thank you aunty."

"You can call me Mrs Nanda," Mother said coldly.

"Okay Mrs Nanda. In any case you don't look old enough to be called aunty—I was quite hesitant to address you so. You've maintained yourself rather well. Honestly Malvika, your mother is very smart."

Naina finalised our rendezvous for the next day and got up to leave. I called out to Bedi.

"He'll escort you back. It's very late. Don't go alone." Naina laughed out aloud at my concern, "Many years ago, life had left me all alone. Since then I have fended for myself. A late night or darkness don't affect me—I'll go, don't worry. Good night."

She turned abruptly and was soon lost in the dark stillness of the hills. I made up my mind that I liked her. Meeting Naina had made me want to return from the voiceless world of stagnation I had gradually submerged myself in. I wanted to shake off my inertia, live for my desires and toil towards their achievement.

***

THE PRINCIPAL OF our school, Sister Martha, was a converted Indian Christian nun from the South. An average girl from an ordinary background, who had faced life's most tender moments with the ruthlessness of poverty, that had now become an integral part of her attitude. She was an extremely dry fundamentalist. Her face reflected her temperament and her tendency to overreact at the slightest provocation. I had not been spared of her ire and now she made her dislike of Naina very evident. Hiding her body in the stark black folds of a nun's robes had done nothing to purify her mind or make her sedate or dignified. Her dealings stank of prejudices and biases. She refused to see the other's point of view and had no compassion for the helplessness of ones situation.

I suffered a lot of humiliation from her even though I didn't deserve it. For Sister Martha, the inner suppression was not a serene state of mind, but it was like a barrier between her sense objects and her, which troubled her. Whenever she was cruel to us I used to remember one of the songs Bhupendra used to sing...

"If you cannot love me, beloved.
Forgive me my pain
Do not look askance at me from afar
I will steal back to my corner and sit in the dark
With both hands
I will cover my naked shame
Turn your face from me, beloved, and forgive me my pain."

Suddenly, I thought of the lines…Bhupen and the past—but at the moment all I could see on Sister Martha's face was an ugly dislike (of what?). It was seldom that she liked anyone. She kept aside Naina's newspaper cuttings and magazines which covered Naina's dance performances.

"I am sorry, Nayantara. Who doesn't know about your

lifestyle? You neither married well nor stayed amiably with your husband and then after you divorced him…what a life…you're no less than a call girl. This school caters to children from decent homes. Your image would be most damaging. Haven't we obliged you enough by conceding to admit your daughter to this school? Now let her live in peace—don't visit her so often okay? Is that clear?"

"You have no right to pass judgements on someone's personal life, Miss Martha. Do you know what it is to fend for yourself and two young children? And if your five year-old child contracts leukemia and you don't have enough money to buy milk for him while his so-called industrialist father is busy touring Europe…then you do not think of your image—there is nothing to life but the image of your child's weary suffering face…anyway…thank you." Naina went out in a huff. I walked right behind her but she was unaware of me. She walked barefoot in a blind alley of the past and the unexpected pebbles hurt her. We walked the entire way in silence. Sometimes she clutched at my hand, and sometimes left it abruptly, and went ahead. We crossed Landor Road, and Naina suddenly stopped and sat on the wall of a small wayside bridge. The surrounding shopkeepers stared at us curiously. Naina's attractive personality and unconventional clothes were enough to arouse anyone's curiosity. I feared a small crowd would soon gather around us and led Naina by the hand to a South Indian restaurant across the road. This was my first visit to this neat eating place with its sparsely occupied benches. We took a corner table. Naina was still preoccupied in her own world. A well oiled lad came up to us doubling up his lungi (sarong) on his thighs and tying its lower edge to his waist. We should order something to eat, I thought to myself, it may ease Naina's tension. I recalled how much Mother and I used to lose ourselves in the act of eating after Papa's death.

"Two dosas and some hot-coffee please." The boy took the order and withdrew from our table while Naina continued to sit motionless, staring at nothing. When the food arrived, she pounced on it and swallowed it down as if she had been hungry since many days. She didn't seem quite herself but gradually regained her composure as she sipped the coffee. 'You shouldn't have come with me Malvika. These are your school hours," she blurted out.

"Does it matter—school is on everyday, but I've found a precious friend today."

"I am surprised you find a friend in me. People don't tire of casting their stones at me, they don't even consider me human." She burst into tears.

On quietening down, her face looked pallid with the dried tears still clinging to her cheeks. "I didn't cry out of self pity Malvika—I cried for five-year-old Micky. There was no money for his milk and I was a slave to the evil habits Micky's father had inculcated in me. I was without money or a roof over my head—unemployed and staying in a rented flat. A year after the divorce, I buried my pride and went to beg them to accept the children. Micky was ill and needed specialised treatment which I could not afford. When I approached him for the treatment, he did not bother to step out of his house to hear my mournful appeal. Instead, his mother made an appearance only to call me names—bitch—swine—and to throw me out. And Micky died—the child of a rich and famous family died—for lack of food and medicine, and with him, something inside me also died. My body became a walking, talking Egyptian mummy—a beautiful body without a soul, desire or the inclination to think. I wanted Mandira to live—I was not prepared to lose her at any cost. So I became a bitch—a low grade one for her sake. I started to hunt hotels and look for obliging patrons who were prepared to buy my body. I had no life of my own…it had become a constant switch of role playing. I crushed the self and the pride of my being. I became scared to meet my own eyes.

"This went on till I had collected enough money. I then admitted Mandira to this boarding school and left Bombay for Orissa. I approached my Guru—Sridharan—but he also rejected me. I was accustomed to rejection. I sat outside his doorstep for a week. I hardly ate or drank anything during that week. He finally gave in and taught me a few steps. I was to go back if unable to perfect them within a month.

Malvika, I tied the dancing bells to my feet and never looked back. I would practise the entire day and late into the night and would even forget to eat. I would lose myself body and soul in dancing. I would massage oil on my fatigued body and the bursting veins of my legs to bring back life into them. The payals would dig into my skin and leave sores which I would heal with a paste of turmeric powder. I don't know how many nights and days I spent like this. My Guru accepted me at last, albiet with some reservations. I mastered in two years what most people can't in six. Dancing became an inseparable part of my life. After losing everything, this was the only act that gave me solace. The vacuum was filling up and I felt the stirrings of achievement."

"Will you have some more coffee, Naina?" I asked in an attempt to quieten her outburst, but she was balanced on some lost page of history.

"Malvika, I travelled extensively, gave dance performances, won prizes, acquired money and along with it many kinds of experiences. All these experiences led me to realise one universal truth—that a woman is a body first, then a human being." She gulped down the steaming hot coffee. The boy who had waited on us stared at her in disbelief. He had been enamoured by her attractive personality and was now shaken to see her swallow the near boiling coffee. He ran to the manager of the restaurant and was probably narrating what he had seen in his native tongue. I paid the bill and walked out with Naina towards her home. She lit a cigarette while we strolled. We passed the skating rink and went through Kulri Bazaar. A cinema show had just given over at Rivoli. It was a motley crowd but they all either gave Naina a second look or just stood and stared after us. She had become the cynosure of their eyes. Her figure and appearance were really quite stunning.

Saxena Lodge was situated just after the pavement beyond the club. It had a tiny annexe at the side. Naina guided me towards the two top rooms and escorted me inside. The first of the two rooms that comprised the annexe were entirely covered with jute matting and had a settee in a corner. There were a couple of cane chairs and the room derived its warmth and colour from the bright cushions strewn around it. Wooden shelves fixed on one of the walls had books and brass and bronze artifacts. An exquisitely carved ivory lamp gave off a soft glow to the room. A few potted plants on the floor and about a dozen bonsai on a long coffee table completed the decor. The other room was even more empty and had a durrie spread across the floor with an intricate music system at one end. A massive painting of Natraj (the dancing Shiva) occupied the better part of the wall, and under it, on an engraved brass plate, lay a pair of payals (dancing anklet bells) which seemed to have been placed with utmost reverence. I was touched by the simple yet artistic expressions of the house.

We made ourselves comfortable in the first room. "This is my little world, Malvika. I have bought this flat. I'll be able to live for Mandira in this remote corner of Mother Earth. I had the mistaken notion that no one would know me here. But my past not only accompanies me but precedes me wherever I go. Why is the media always so ruthlessly sensational? It doesn't spare anyone—it cannot understand the pain and constraints of one's situation."

"Forget it Naina, don't be disillusioned. You've had the courage to reach till here; you're sure to go ahead from here too. You should be proud of your achievements. Today has been a good excuse to know all about you and understand you better."

"Yes, I think I wasn't quite in my senses. I used you as a confession box and detailed all the gory events of my life leaving nothing in reserve."

"Make me your permanent confession box Naina. Whenever you want to lessen your burdens or unburden yourself you are welcome to do so without any reservations, okay?"

"Okay…" Naina seemed relaxed now. Mother's concern broke into annoyance the minute she saw me, "Where have you been all this while? You generally come back at two o'clock from school."

"I went to Naina's house."

"That's a lot of friendship cemented in one day."

"Yes, it often happens that way, Mother. Friendships are formed in a day or not at all."

"I don't ever remember any of your friends visiting you when you were young—except for Savita. I wonder what she is doing now. We never kept track of any one—how many years has it been since we went to Delhi."

"Five years. And Savita was married when we were still at Delhi. She must be the mother of children by now."

"Really," mother pondered over that and then said, "Who is this Naina? I've never seen such an attractive looking creature. She's dark but has a peculiar charm about her. What a perfect figure...."

"She's an expert dancer Mother...she's divorced. Her daugther is in my school."

"Is that so...she doesn't look married or the mother of a kid."

"Her daughter is twelve years old...."

"Really," Mother peered into the mirror above the reception table and examined her own face. "But there is something I must say Malvika. Your friend is just like you. She has no table manners."

"So what? She has gone beyond the surface of life and has a deep understanding of it. She has had to pay heavily with experiences to attain this."

"What's that?" Mother was perplexed at this.

"No, nothing. Don't bother your head over such

things. How many people in India have a table to attain the manners for it and what's wrong in eating the Indian way? Why must we continue to live a life that is unsuitable to the environment around us? If a borrowed living trend is manners—then I can't help ridiculing it...."

"Okay, let's forget this. You'll never understand, it's the effect of the Indian rituals Bhaiji has taught you to perform...chanting mantras and prayers...all for what? Anyway, he's coming tomorrow with a foreign tourist. He's written that he is a French artist. I don't know how we are going to make him comfortable in this off season. Our bearers are quite ignorant of the subtleties of gracious serving."

"Don't get worried, Mother. You constantly make an issue out of table manners. These foreigners neither have servants nor bearers to serve them in their houses. They do all their chores themselves—from washing the dishes to cleaning the loo. It's our own feeling of inadequancy that makes us hero worship white skinned people. Just relax and try to lead a simple life without any hassles or pretensions."

"Alright, let's hope for the best and see how things shape out." Mother had made an attempt to end the conversation but I knew she would keep thinking about the French artist.

***

IT WAS A Sunday. Janaki was clearing up the garden with Bedi's help. While pruning the trees she was singing a song.

It was a song of hiccups. Hiccups are said to indicate that someone who loves you is thinking of you.

Janaki sang:

"Days have gone by
Since last I saw you
Months have passed
Since we were together
And still my love
You are so far away
Oh these hiccups
I think my darling
Is longing for me
The grains of my youth and beauty
Are being pecked away
By the bird of time
I warned you
Not to leave me
Oh these hiccups
I think my darling
Is longing for me."

"What is this word Sapadi?" I wanted to know.

"Don't you know Sapadi? It means guava."

"Look over there, Uncle's car has arrived."

I went towards the gate. He was accompanied by that French artist.

"Meet Pierre, your new guest. Pierre, this is my niece

Malvika. She is studying for her PhD—a student of psychology."

Pierre folded his hands and said Namaskar.

I was impressed.

"Do girls in India go in for higher education?"

He spoke in Hindi and his accent was remarkably good.

"Pierre has been in India since the past two years and has learnt Hindi rather well."

"Yes," I said.

Pierre was an ordinary looking Frenchman of average height. Bhaiji told me that his interest in History, Art and Painting had brought him to India. We crossed the garden and ascended to the verandah. Mother was waiting for us at the reception. Bhaiji made the necessary introductions, "But you don't look like her mother," Pierre said. "I've yet to meet such a graceful lady in India." He kissed mother's hand with a special graciousness.

Mother was obviously pleased with this remark and felt encouraged to take the visitor in to see Nirmal Kunj. Bhaiji and I waited outside and he asked after my various activities—the school, the field work required for my thesis and also about Mother. He seemed more relaxed than he had been on his earlier visits. Perhaps like us, he had gained confidence in our growing self dependence. Just then, I heard Mother's voice beckoning me to come inside.

Bhaiji and I saw Pierre gazing intently at one of the

paintings. "Do you know who is the artist of this painting Malvika?" Mother asked.

"No," I said. "The artist's name had been erased from the faded landscape."

"This painting has been here since ages," Bhaiji said.

"As far as I remember, Father had brought back two or three like this one from one of his trips abroad. I took one to Dehradun. I don't know what became of the others."

"Yes, it is ancient. It could be a Monet. It has the same style and medium. It probably has a lot of antique value."

"Really?" Mother expressed her surprise, "I wonder why these discoloured, dirty old knick-knacks fetch so much money."

"Do you know when man developed a taste for buying old things and how they were rendered valuable?"

"No," I was also curious to know what Pierre had to say.

"In the beginning there was the King and there were his people. Only the king had the right or the ability to buy expensive articles and maintain them. But gradually when great wars and battles were fought, Kingships came to an end. The common man earned enough money and developed the capacity to build his house like a palace. In fact, he fashioned the decor of his luxurious house on the ancient palaces. His ego was greatly satisfied to think that he could buy the very same stuff that once graced the royal rooms. It was like a triumph over royalty—and so the 'antique' was born."

"You've explained it very lucidly."

"After all, he's an artist himself," said Bhaiji.

"No wonder you know so much about Art," I said.

"Why don't you come and see your room?" Mother interrupted. Pierre had been allotted the corner room on the first floor. One could view the back of the town from there—the steep slopes of the hillsides where there were no houses and the pine fir trees on the terraces of the slopes. From the eastern window, one could see the winding road that went up to the Savoy. We had reached Pierre's room and Janaki had placed the tea tray on the table.

All at once there was a deafening screech as a colony of bats made their way from one of the pine trees and flapped their wings against the window pane.

"Good Lord," said Janaki, "what a bad omen. It's twilight and these bats are screaming...and today is Thursday...."

"Go about your work Janaki," Mother said, dismissing her from the room, fearing she might come out with some juicy story, or sensational memory from the history of Nirmal Kunj.

Naina was trying to make me laugh but I could not be shaken out of my depression. I had spoilt the report of my field work and had a fruitless argument with Sharatji over it. He had suggested that I should spend some time in Delhi. My data would be incomplete without field work in a metropolis. The mention of Delhi had been enough to put me off. Naina was in a jocular mood and was talking of her experiences abroad. "Do you know Malvika, there is a fisherman's paradise—Baltimore—in America. I once met a woman there who had wedded seven times. It worked out to a ratio of one wedding a year, so I asked her, 'You haven't got married this year?' and she said, 'I didn't want to ruin my summer holidays." Naina was in splits of laughter.

"People never seem to tire of getting married, fighting, resorting to physical violence, giving birth to children and then separating. They make a mockery of marriage."

"The body has its own language—but most people do not want to understand it. They only wish to own the body by any means. So marriage becomes a licence to torture your wife, to rape her, without having anyone lift a finger against you. And the scotchtape of enduring relationship seals your lips."

"Naina, is the body really so important that its consuming language can engulf a man to annihilate his intellect?"

"Yes—I have experienced the passion for this body in many different ways. Naresh had a perverted approach. You understand masochism. Psychology is your subject."

"Yes...tormenting oneself and the other while in the process of achieving sexual gratification. You can call such a person a sadist—a person who enjoys inflicting ingenuously designed pain on the other partner."

"Yes...staying with Naresh, I became used to tolerating the pain inflicted on me. He had a strange madness in him that would find its roughest (brutal) expression on me, leaving me also abnormal in the process. I had to suffer in silence under the circumstances and because of the presence of the children. Then one day, he threw me out perhaps because I had stopped reacting the way he wanted me to. I was a lifeless soul in a fatigued body, that just breathed somehow. What he desired was violence, and my screams—a terror stricken woman who could satiate his thirst....." Naina had unshed tears in her eyes.

"So, I came away. I had a small flat...two children...no money and a broken spirit in an abused body. I made no headway when I begged for a job—any job. My begging bowl was neither made up of a college degree nor a beautiful body. I could not possibly have restarted my studies at that stage. So I turned to the next best thing. I started working on my body like a project. I read books on the subject, did yogic exercises, underwent diets and massage. I carved my body till I was sure no man could resist from desiring it. I felt as if Cupid himself dwelt in it and it happened."

All this was quite strange and new to me and I felt a little afraid of Naina. I said, "But Naina, why did you do a thing like that—what did you achieve?"

"My body had become my strength. I had nothing besides

it. I just wanted to live a complete life. I can now trap any man with my magical attraction and make him do exactly what I want. My body has become the source of my energy and a tool to earn money. But I am not cheap, Malvika. I am completely disciplined—viewing this new energy of mine with objectivity and putting it to new tests and experiments."

I couldn't help staring at her for there was some truth in what she said. For the first time, I felt that there was nothing non-dignified in sex. It has been given a mysterious colour by people who don't understand the desire. It had nothing cheap or gross in it. For the first time, I felt no revulsion towards sex. It had been made indecorous by closeting and thwarting its natural feelings. I felt the sweet pangs of my only distant stolen kiss. It was my most treasured memory, worthy of worship and whenever I relived that moment, it gave me inner peace, as if I was chanting a divine name to the beads of a rosary.

"Malvika you have never disclosed anything about your love affair?"

"There is nothing to disclose."

"Come, there must be something."

"I don't know if it was an attachment, love or merely the infatuation of youth. But, whatever it was, it has hurt me deeply."

"Anything that hurts has to be genuine." Naina poured the tea. "Actually we are never able to assess ourselves or our feelings—and without discovering ourselves, we make vital decisions in life. You could have asked him what he found lacking in you?"

"Where was the time to ask him? Papa had just died... and on his funeral pyre, my love was also burnt."

"Well if you have burnt it, then you should forget about it. But don't tell me you did not find any one else all these years?"

"No. I did not find anyone else—there is no one here—and the ones who do come...I only view them as tourists. They are here today and will soon be gone...getting lost in the world."

"All of them are not tourists...and everyone doesn't have to be gone."

"But I don't feel any kind of desire or love within me, Naina. Everything is like one large supermarket where various items are very attractively packaged and displayed—but we either don't have the inclination for most things or don't need them—so I don't even bother to look around."

"But this won't do! The body is beautiful and needs the fulfilment of experience—full of vigour and intoxication. I think I'll have to do something—you were talking about a French artist the other day...What's he like?"

"Like any artist—trying to seek the depths of all that he views."

"And how does he view you?" Naina asked in a naughty voice.

"I know I am no inspiration for an artist's imagination."

The rain had quickened its pace outside. I had better leave the moment it slowes down, I thought, or Bedi would soon come looking for me.

"Let's listen to some Rabindra Sangeet—it's ideal for this kind of weather."

"Why do you always like to listen to Rabindra Sangeet, Malvika?"

"Listen to it Naina—you will yourself understand why."

It was very late—incessant work at the laboratory had me fatigued completely with a backache. But Sharatji was busy drawing lines on a graph paper with red and green pencils with intense concentration. I wondered how this man never got tired—or thought of packing up early and going home. His eyes had sunk into their sockets with the strain of concentration. His hands, eyes, mind always seemed preoccupied with work. A quest paper to be prepared or a topic from a new book would soon become the object of his working. Sharatji never took a holiday. His handy lab assistant would provide him the required flow of sandwiches, tea or cigarettes, and once even medicines which he entrusted me to give every six hours to Sharatji. The lab boy informed me, "Professor Sahib's wife stays in the village. She's a total rustic and doesn't even know how to converse. She came over here once with their son—a lanky brat who cannot talk without using foul language and constantly picks up fights.

They went back to the village after unsuccessful attempts to educate him, and have never come back since; nor does Sahib go to visit them. A dutiful money order is sent every month."

Sharatji never talked about himself. In the three years that I had been here, he had never told me anything about himself. Whatever he writes is an integral part of him. On the other hand, a Platonist doesn't even have the courage to think openly about himself. He wants others to understand him from his real performance. A psychologist is no different—he lives the experience of the people he analyses.

"What are you thinking about, Malvika? You have been sitting very quietly—have you got your data wrong?"

"No, Sir...I was just wondering what a psychologist is made up of—doesn't he have anything non-organic about him? Is he only like a zero of no value in itself but capable of carrying the statistics of the data?"

"No, I don't think so. A psychologist is a human being too, although leading a life different from the normal one. He is forced to treat human relationships like the parts of a machine. Circumstances weaken him. Most middle class families don't have an intellectual approach in their behaviour. Their life is confined within the walls of household obligations...which means brain death...."

"I am surprised to hear you saying a thing like that, Sir."

"Yes I am saying it because where I stand, life and

intellectualism or art (call it anything) can destroy each other. I cannot help fearing such a possibility. This fear takes away the joy from happiness. The fear of my failing to adjust to a rural life prevents me from going back to my wife."

"Why don't you try and improve the situation...at least you can rise above this fear...tell me about it...talking to someone may have a cathartic effect."

"I am afraid I cannot improve the situation in any way. Only a miracle can save me. I lead an intellectual life in a petty repose, in the hope that something spectacular will occur one day. Intellectualism believes that progress will lead to a marvel—but your desires prevent anything spectacular or marvellous to occur. I also realise that a belief in miracles is the refuge of the religious minded person, not of one leading a practical life. But there seems to be a curse on me. What have I done to deserve this—why did I not attain a complete existence?"

"Do you think anyone else has attained it. Is any one complete in this world?"

But Sharatji was like a river in spate. "If God won't pay heed to my struggle to attain a complete existence then I will bang my head on the threshold of intellectualism and destroy it."

I stepped back in fear—I had never seen Sharatji like this—what had come over him? I felt that anyone waiting for a miracle to occur in his life was only inviting mishaps.

The more I tried to understand him the more I got entangled in the confusion. The unintelligibility attached to his intellectualism had devastated his thinking and could only lead his desolate journey to nothingness, to nowhere.

Pierre had become very friendly with the family. Ma was looking after him extremely well. She acquired new crockery and cutlery for Nirmal Kunj. Food was also cooked with great interest and care. It was mainly western cuisine. But Pierre's manners rather startled me more than Ma. He made a lot of noise while drinking his soup and drank it to the last drop. He even chewed his chicken lifting it with his fingers. He hardly used a fork or knife. He showed total disregard for the so called dictionary of manners, yet he imparted a politeness towards us which no other guest of ours had have shown. He would not allow Bedi to serve him before us in the usual order of succession at the table. He even enjoyed Janki's language and folk songs.

Pierre was mainly a landscape painter; occasionally he did portraits. He carried with him an album of colour plates he had painted so far, and a collection of some books on art. After having a few solo exhibitions of his paintings in Paris he had come to India. He showed me lots of press notes and paper cuttings which talked highly of his art. Most of the critics compared his work to 'Monet', who was a great landscape painter of France. I was not too familiar with art or artists but I enjoyed Pierre's work. He mainly painted outdoors. He was happy to be in Nirmal Kunj. He liked the house, its atmosphere, the garden. Weather was favourable and he was well looked after. He was quite talkative but at times silent and withdrawn, and sometimes incoherent and rambling.

Pierre never spoke much of his personal life. He had divorced his wife and considered marriage a commodity fit for hatred, a useless tie which converts a person into a boring and dry human being. However, he never expressed much feeling for his childhood or family other than his aunt Margret, who was a painter herself. He talked about her with great regard, although she viewed her nephew's paintings as hopeless. Pierre talked about various things—it was like weaving a picture. He never passed judgements on people; he only implied his opinion of them by the soft tone of voice. He would talk of the difficult periods in his life calmly and without regret. He talked about the bohemian world of Paris, artists of every calibre, good and bad. A few months before his arrival in India Pierre had held an exhibition of paintings of scenes from India. He showed me the favourable reviews he had got, all neatly filed. The printed reproductions of his paintings were quite realistic. He had captured nature in all her moods and colours.

"Pierre how do you manage to reproduce nature so well on your canvases? Don't you get tired of painting various aspects of nature all the time?"

"You know what Monet said about nature, Malvika? He claimed that he had painted the river Siene in all its various moods. He used to say that he never got tired of it and that it appeared different to him everytime he viewed it. Staying so close to nature made Monet feel exhilarated everytime he saw the sun rise and depressed when he saw it setting. He commenced his work with the changing hues of light—not in a studio but out in the open and would often leave his incomplete canvas late at night and would start painting again at the crack of dawn. If you think of it, the first faint light at the break of dawn barely catches the dewdrops on the flowers and leaves—Monet's palette would enfold that moment in its colours, and enliven it for all time on his canvas He was also fond of painting reflections in the water."

"We live on by what we achieve in the process of living. Monet has not only enlivened and immortalised nature but himself on his canvases," I said, now deeply involved in understanding art. "So much for Monet—what about your own works, Pierre—tell me something more about them."

"My earlier works were more experimental. I would decorate my colourful backgrounds with lines and dots, playfully placing them as if they were toys. But coming to India changed all that. The background of my painting always had a great significance for me—now even the overlying sketches have achieved a crucial importance. There is so much diversity in this country. There are so many shades in the almond colour complexions of Indian women, and what a variety of expressions! Faces—contorted in pain and suffering, or twisted in an inhibited sensuality or simply blank. I have never seen such blank resignation anywhere else in the world. That's why I come here so often. I have been coming every year for the past six years. I stay in small towns and paint my pictures. Every state in India has its own special landscape; nature expresses herself so differently in each place—that's what fascinates me about this country, Malvika."

I had now started to appreciate Art. I was able to understand Pierre's paintings. His obsessive interest in nature was obviously a subconscious reliving and a fixation for Monet. He didn't paint his landscape like photographs, but had a distinct impressionistic style. The hillsides he painted, the wild flowers amidst tall grass, pine trees, goats coming down a slope, the rainbow, waters of a river shimmering in the sunrise or sunset—all transported the viewer to the shores of the River Seine. I would tire of only scenes and ask Pierre… "But don't we need a foil or antithesis in order to realise anything?"

"Not always. Sometimes cruel events and hideous objects become immortal by the perfect representation of their perfect ugliness. So the antithesis you are looking for does not remain an antithesis but becomes a logical picturisation in its own right. Art has a habit of recreating all that is not actually visible to our naked eye."

'You mean, the invisible becomes enigmatic?"

"No, Malvika, after all we need a penetratingly suspicious insight to look into ourselves too. Our day to day experiences have no totality about them. But somewhere along the way, there are also our dreams and desires, which are not very clearly visible. Art is the attempt to straighten and lay bare, all our hidden, warped feelings which do not surface easily. The creation of the artist becomes the honest expression of his quintessential qualities and moods."

"Okay, suppose he does give a form to the manifestation of his inner self—but what if it conveys nothing to the viewer—what if it does not reach us?"

"Then his art becomes lifeless—it is like a dead body. Art should revolutionise your thinking—it has to be rebellious, breaking all boundaries and engulfing the viewer with its expression."

"Where can one see such paintings these days? Today art is wrapped up in formula. I think society is the loser when the artist fails to make the intended impact with his communication. Don't you think the artists of today try to romanticise the past like historians or archaeologists. They try to establish a relationship between the past and the present, where none actually exists. And even if we get involved with what the artist tries to communicate to us the involvement is momentary."

"Do you then think that the future is only imagination? A Gestalt—which is made up of non-existent forms? Can't art be the resultant reaction to all that lies within you and be very personal?"

"Well, actually anything that is communicated through poetry, music or an image is the expression of our inner self. So many places of worship have the idols of Buddha or Christ, but the peace and sublimity in the Padampani Buddha of Ajanta, the Tathagat of Sarswati or the Crucifixtion of Giaho are beyond compare. Art is like a miracle. The keen intellect and intensity of the artist reaches out for something that has been lost in oblivion and recreates it into a tangible image."

***

BEDI WANTED TO take Mother to a holy shrine high up in the hills but she always rejected the idea. When he would insist, she'd say "No Bedi, I don't think I will go. What's the point in worshipping a lifeless stone?" Bedi would explain, "It's an important shrine. All your wishes are granted if you visit it once—at least you could give it a try."

That day, perhaps encouraged by some strange apprehension, she changed her mind and agreed. My convent-educated mother—so Western in thought and action had decided to visit a holy shrine.

Bedi turned to me, "Why don't you also come along, Didiji... there can be no salvation till one has undertaken this pilgrimage."

I smiled. "Bedi, do you think it's for worship that people go there facing all the hardships en-route?"

"Of course," he retorted.

Janakl tended to concur. "Oh, you must go Bitto Didi; everyone in this family has made the journey...even Johar Bai, who could hardly be called a believer, used to go there."

"An educated woman like her? Was she religious too?"

What could I say? That we actually visit a temple to worship our inner fears. Man has always nursed his most intimate truths in remote, desolate places. I agreed finally, attracted by the prospect of the trek. Pierre came along too, with his sketchbooks, pencils and a camera.

We passed through the narrow lanes of a village on our way. On either side were shabby and squalid hutments. I wondered how people managed to survive in such inhospitable environs. It was cold but all the children were naked and carefree, dirty and mud-bespattered but with bright and shiny faces. Further ahead on one side of the goat track there was a sharp drop to the bottom of the valley. Oblivious to such dangers, the kids played with wild abandon. Mother could not help remarking, "Amazing, isn't it? How can one be so unaffected by the fear of death?"

"I agree," said Pierre.

"They do seem to be on a tightrope. . . but there's danger everywhere...even when you are leading a sheltered life. Don't you think that the innocence and spontaneity of childhood are then destroyed?"

"The children of our country are indeed unfortunate, Malvika. Our childhood is spent in seclusion or at best, with a baby-sitter or a nanny. The parents are busy working at bettering their prospects and setting up homes. Children get affection in bits and pieces or not at all. These children are poor no doubt but at least they are happy and healthy. They get looked after by their parents, are fed at the breast rather than from a bottle. Everyone eats together. The intimacy bred thus is surely healthier than the most nutritious of foods."

Mother kept walking on in silence while Pierre stopped to take some photographs. Bedi hurried us on before Pierre could get down to some sketching.

Finally, we reached the temple, which was in a state of disrepair and neglect but the idols swere intricately carved. The portals of black wood were held together by brass nails, set off by a resplendent brass disc.

"How beautiful...." Pierre was speechless with admiration. "Please do not touch anything...you foreigner!" A man emerged out of one of the dark caverns of the hall.

"I am a human being, no foreigner...." The man was taken aback by such chaste Hindi.

"Oh I am sorry, I thought..." he turned his gaze upon me as if he knew me. He somehow seemed familar. He did not look like a priest—glowing with good health. He was tall and had a prominent forehead with a sandalwood paste 'tilak'. He did not appear to be more than thirty-five years of age. Dressed in a dhoti and a sheer upper shawl, his distinguished personality exuded some kind of a strange magnetism. Bidding us enter, he led us through a small courtyard. The open door of a small room revealed innumerable books kept meticulously. What is this soft-spoken saint doing hibernating here, I wondered. Bedi beckoned Mother to stand before the idol. It was a Ganesha statue, trunk curled upwards, made of what appeared to be black stone. Why should such a finely adorned statue be tucked away in obscurity—almost as if someone had concealed it from the prying eyes of the world.

The priest made Mother sit down before the idol and started conducting religious rites by chanting mantras. Bedi joined them in the proceedings. I witnessed their reactions and held the flood of silent questions within me with the detachment of a tourist.

Bedi beckoned to me when they had finished their prayer and I walked over.

"Are you married?" queried the priest, looking at me with his beautiful eyes.

"No." I was taken aback.

"Oh! she is still a child," Mother said.

"Not really," the priest persisted.

"Early marriages are not possible in families of high

status, Swamiji," Bedi shielded Mother from any further questions.

He then handed me a banana leaf on which were some grains of rice, vermillion, betel nuts and a betel leaf and started muttering incoherently. It sounded very familiar. Something my uncle had taught me when I was a child. It all came back now and I was fascinated. Just then Pierre asked the priest something about the temple.

He told us how one of the yogis, Bhrigu Muni, attacked Vishnu the God on his chest. This was done to test the trinity. His wife Lakshmi did not like this and decided to go away to Baikunth. Large-hearted God Vishnu had forgiven Bhrigu Muni because he felt that one must forgive the person who has made a mistake. But their son Ganesh could not take Lakshmi's separation so he left his father's home. Since then, this place has been his abode. When Lakshmi heard about this she came to visit him in the form of a cow. Ganeshji was living in the cave and she would shower milk over the cave so that he was fed properly. This is the reason why Ganeshji's trunk is turned upwards to gather milk, and his complexion is dark because he lived in a cave. That very cave was converted into a temple. "So much time has gone by, so many changes have taken place but this temple remained undamaged." Pierre and I were listening intently. Pierre was scribbling furiously in his diary.

"Ever since I was a child I have been an ardent admirer

of Michelangelo's work," said Pierre. "During my childhood I came in contact with a lot of people who had witnessed the Second World War. They had all kinds of mixed reactions to it. Some believed that it was a punishment for mankind and caused much destruction while others thought that it actually put an end to the old and decrepit, to make room for nascence. War, they thought, disciplined and reformed evil."

The priest joined in, "I have not seen much of the outside world but from what I have read I have come to believe that every life symbolizes a struggle, an internal battle that constantly wages inside each of us."

Pierre concurred, but queried, "Yes, but can it really be compared with the Great Wars?"

"We Indians even talk about emerging victorious in this battle as a form of religion. The kind of religion that liberates the soul and even makes one prosperous. In the usual wars we are dependent on arms, but internal battles are fought against the five senses. Our religion is the weapon used in this war. The mind is the commander who can discipline the senses at will, and win the battle."

"Yes, one has to rely on weapons to win a war. So we rely on God or religion—that is probably the only difference..."

The priest and Pierre had taken to each other and I found it rather interesting. Mother rested outside on a platform. "Swamiji, have you heard...?"

"You can call me Roshan. I have not renounced the world

as yet. I am but a student," said the priest.

"Okay Roshan, have you heard about the idol that has been found in a Hindu temple at Bangkok? The most amazing thing is that it is naked above the waist. Over the shoulder, in place of the sacred thread, is a snake. I am quite fond of doing comparative studies of Western and Indian icons."

"Are you doing this research merely to satisfy your own interest?"

"Not quite. I plan to write a book. Sometime back I came across an ancient book from Hanoi. In it were many photographs of Indian idols. Some of the ornaments on the idol are easily visible in India today."

"I have also read somewhere about Red Indians in Mexico worshipping a deity with the head of an elephant, bearing a striking resemblance to Ganesha..." I interjected.

The priest expressed surprise, "That's amazing. I had no idea at all that Ganesha was worshipped abroad."

Bedi called out to us. "I think we should make a move now."

The priest was loathe to leave us. "Why don't you stay a while. It's ages since I have had someone educated to talk to in this remote and desolate place."

"Why don't you visit us at Mussoorie?"

"You must give me the address. The priest rummaged about for some paper.

Bedi tried to cut things short. "It's very simple and rather well known, Nirmal Kunj, Camel Back Road…there."

"What…Nirmal Kunj?"

"Why are you disturbed to hear the name Nirmal Kunj?" Bedi asked. The priest's face was ashen. "The concubine does not live there anymore. It's a hotel now." Roshan turned his face away.

"Do visit us, Roshan. I am here for a few more months," Pierre implored. But Roshan vanished into one of the dark caverns without bidding us farewell. We set out.

"Strange! Why did he clamp up suddenly?" Pierre found it peculiar.

"You certainly took ages." Mother's reproachful tone indicated that she resented the newfound intimacy between Pierre and me.

"You should have been there, Vinni. It was an interesting conversation. He was even educated…."

Mother did not want to get involved in any argument. "Let's eat something, I am famished."

"There can be nothing more profound than that, Vinni." He held Mother in his arms and the two of them slid down on to the rug Bedi had spread for us.

"Vinni?" I was shocked. This was how father used to address Mother. How did Pierre know?

Mother spread out a clean table cloth and set the cutlery meticulously. We sat down to a hearty meal of sandwiches, boiled eggs and cake. I distractedly picked up an apple and nibbled on it.

"Why don't you have something?" Bedi remarked.

"I am not hungry," I replied.

Mother shot me a glance and turned to Bedi, "You must have something. It would be night by the time we reach home."

"No Memsahib, we do not eat non-vegetarian food after a pilgrimage."

Mother did not reply. She started to peel another boiled egg.

There was a great hue and cry when we returned home. It was only Janaki who could create such a scene. She was screeming at the top of her voice.

"Why are you upset? What's the matter?" I chided.

"I cannot tell you."

"Go on, tell her, you don't have to be so protective about your husband. Tell her what brought you to..." Bedi's anger was quite evident.

"Quit beating about the bush, what has happened?" Janaki wailed louder still.

Bedi had to explain, "That rascal of her husband has brought home a young girl—such a disgrace to have a minor for his mistress."

Janaki wailed even louder.

"This man must be handed over to the police. Janaki

send the girl back to her home. Kishen Lal is getting quite out of hand."

"No, Bibiji, let's not bring the police in."

"You must be out of your mind. He has ruined a girl's life and you still want to shield him."

"Shut up," Janaki could no longer let Bedi talk about her husband.

"Janaki, it's because you keep defending him that he has performed this degrading act. Why do you want to cover up his weaknesses. He is good for nothing. He ill treats you and now this scandal."

"Bibiji, he is still my husband... I am helpless..."

"Nonsense. It is people like you who instigate and encourage husbands to do whatever they want. Don't you realize that there's no crime more heinous than abducting a young girl? We must hand him over to the police."

Just then the Chowkidar came and announced, "Bitto Didi, a Sahib and memsahib have come to see you."

"Show them in." I could see a middle aged couple at the gate. I instructed Bedi to get the girl away from Kishen Lal and not let him escape. This really was the last straw.

Pierre agreed whole-heartedly. "He should not be spared. He ought to be given severe punishment for doing this to a minor. Rape is a far more serious crime than murder."

Janaki kept pleading with us to spare her husband.

"Please forgive him this one time..."

'You will never learn, or realize how wicked your husband is."

"That's truly the problem with most people. We learn so slowly and thus our whole world rests squarely on lies and deceit."

Meanwhile, the old couple had entered. They looked quite respectable. Thinking that they had come to stay at Nirmal Kunj, I took over. They seemed infinitely sad. They sat in silence for a while, probably at a loss for words. Finally they revealed that they were from Delhi and asked for Kishen Lal.

"He doesn't work here."

"And Janaki Devi?"

"Oh yes, she does, why?"

"Kishen Lal, her brother has kidnapped our daughter." They were embarrassed.

"What? He is not her brother but her husband. Are you sure that he has kidnapped her? It's also possible that she was willing to elope with him."

They kept quiet.

"How did you meet Kishen Lal?" I asked the couple.

"He used to supply antiques to our shop 'Art Palace'. He would visit our shop very frequently. Our daughter used to help out at the shop. Little did we know that he would abduct her.... We finally managed to get hold of his address from another shopkeeper and here we are. Where is she? We do hope she is fine."

I was livid with rage. First this messy kidnapping and now the mystery of the disappearance of the antiques of Nirmal Kunj was finally solved. Bedi brought the girl over. She was an impudent looking girl, barely fifteen or sixteen, with a body that belied her age. She did not look nervous or embarrassed or even repentant. She somehow reminded me of Naina. She had a vulgar voluptuosness about her. She stood impassively before her parents, as if nothing extraordinary had happened.

Her mother burst out, "You wicked slut! Aren't you ashamed of yourself?" She even slapped the girl.

"We'll take care of her once we get home—she needs straightening out," the father interjected.

"We'll take your leave now, we are eternally grateful to you for all your help."

I was horrified. "Aren't you going to hand him over to the police? He must not be left scotfree. That would only encourage him more."

"Oh no. It would ruin our daughter's reputation. Every one has been told that she has gone visiting her grandmother."

"This is outrageous. You are sensible people. I don't know why you advocate taking no action against the rascal. Is it right to let him go unpunished? Rape is a serious crime."

"Our hands are tied. There is no use going to the police.

Even if they do take some action, there would be much publicity which we cannot go through. Besides, when we realize that our daughter connived with him, there's little hope." The father was literally in tears. Her mother remained unmoved.

I turned to the girl, "And what do you have to say about all this?"

She giggled, "It was such a thrilling adventure. He is fun. The whole idea seemed so exciting. Anyway, who are you to demand an explanation? This is a personal matter and I don't wish to discuss it with you." Her tone became arrogant and her eyes hardened.

It was my turn to be stunned. Such audacity! How dare she question my authority. "Please leave the hotel premises at once," I trembled with an impotent rage. "Bedi turn these people out and Kishen Lal too. Instruct the guard not to ever let him in again. Go and fetch Janaki."

I exploded when I saw her. "Janaki, with whose permission did you sell off the articles of this house? Just tell me the truth." Janaki tried to deny the charge.

"I am warning you. Either you make a clean breast of things or you will go to jail along with Kishen Lal."

She finally confessed, "We sold some old things from the store. But they were hardly of any use. They were all broken. Why don't you ask Kishen Lal?"

"I refuse to see him. Just tell him that if there's anything unsold, he will be suitably rewarded if he returns it."

"There's only a piano at Mr David's that can be sent for. That's the only thing of value," she added, rather thoughtful.

"All right. And now you listen…if I ever set eyes on that sordid husband of yours, he'll have to face serious consequences. Is that quite clear?"

"Why should we even touch anything, Didiji? For years we have looked after everything with so much care."

"That's enough. I want to hear no further about this."

"But he is my husband, Didiji. How can I..."

"Be off with you now." And she went away muttering to herself, sounding disgruntled.

I called Bedi and sent him over to Mr David's house to get the piano back. God knows what else had been lost out of such valuable family possessions.

Mother returned presently and was quite upset about Kishen Lal and on being told about the pilferage.

"Kishen Lal has to be taught a lesson. He is getting worse day by day. I have told Janaki that she is welcome to quit anytime if she doesn't like staying here alone. And that girl was the limit. Utterly shameless."

"Really, I was shocked at her behaviour," Pierre broke in, "I don't know why you have to be so worked up over all this. It's perfectly normal. At a certain age, adolescent boys and girls get engulfed in feelings about the opposite sex. No obstacle is insurmountable for one who is consumed with such sensuous desires. Everything appears to be a delectable mystery which is such a thrill to unravel. In our country there are hardly any prohibitions after the age of twelve or thirteen."

This did sound strange to me. Can one be so totally obsessed by the desires of the flesh so as to abandon ones sense of propriety? I remembered my first step into this world with Bhupen—it was so innocent and pure. It was totally disjointed from all this grossness. Bedi poured out the tea for us. Mother got up after she had finished. "Let's go for a walk," she said

"That a great idea. Such lovely weather! Why don't you come along too, Malvika? To hell with Kishen Lal and Janaki," Pierre exclaimed.

"No, she has to look into the accounts," Mother had decided things for me already. She had a rather uncaring and indifferent look on her face—something almost as mysterious as that on the girl's face. I turned and went in disregarding Mother completely. There was a stange turmoil going on inside me. Human nature is so strange, all our troubles are born out of its unreliability. It can hardly ever be predicted. Even the simplest of things get transformed into the most complicated of problems. It's almost as if it was the primary purpose of our nature to create such irritants—somewhat as natural as a tree having leaves. However, if one deliberately suspended such faculties, one became absolutely peaceful.

There were some of his water colours kept outside Pierre's room. He would first paint them and then wash them over. They looked misty and faded and had a surreal dream-like quality about them. I gazed at them for long. I was struck with an overwhelming feeling of being all alone. It seemed to me as if lonelines was felt most when one element of ones being was trying to triumph over another. It is a kind of incompleteness that emanates from within and gradually spreads without and manifests in a frozen moment, somewhat awe struck by the grandeur of the outside world. Pierre's paintings were redolent of this solitude. One portrayed a woman with a full body but rather vacant eyes. She seemed to be somewhat like Mother. There was a vacant chair next to her, probably for me or my negligible existence, I thought.

Suddenly Pierre had beckoned me rather softly.

"Hey listen!"

"Oh, I didn't want to disturb you while you were painting. But you've hardly done anything .... the canvas is unblemished."

"I'm not like you. You're always busy doing something... school, studies....looking after the accounts...."

"What can I do? It just has to be done. Never mind though! What about you, why aren't you working?"

"Sometimes one doesn't feel like painting on canvas. You know I love to paint on the human body especially on the breasts. Firm breasts provide a mountainous landscape...." I was quite taken aback by such frightful candour.

"God, Pierre, there is a limit to joking."

"No, I am extremely serious. In our society it's not so improbable to organise."

"This is hardly your society and I have nothing to do with all this," was all I could manage to say before rushing out.

Janaki had once explained to me, "This house has a curse on it. First a concubine lived here and now a widow. No married woman can feel safe or secure of her status. And you just don't seem to be the type to get married. God alone knows what's going to happen to this household and the women who live under this roof."

***

THE TOPIC OF my research was "The Effects of Stress On Mental Health." I was to question whether day-to-day insignificant events added up in forging our overall behaviour—a research into the somewhat darker recesses of human nature. Such influences at times distort or even totally destroy our personality. Mental pressure is often more potent than the strain of the physical world.

Sharatji wanted me to travel to cosmopolitan cities, specially Delhi. I would have to collect data by interviewing about two hundred people. The strains and tensions of living were probably more seriously felt in a metropolis like

Delhi. The schools had closed down for the winter break. There hadn't been any snowfall but every morning one could make out the all pervading whiteness of the frozen dew on the vegetation. Mother and Pierre chose to stay back in Mussoorie. Sharatji was to present a paper on "Stress and Counter Pressures" at one of the seminars to be held in Delhi.

I had received a letter from Naina from Bombay. She was to be soon back in Delhi after a three month tour of Europe. Maybe we could get to meet. I'd be leaving Mussoorie after six years. The old memories came flooding back. My days with Papa, the house we lived in, the sweet and sour memories of my student days engulfed me. I could almost hear Bhupen telling me, "Malvika, you are my closest friend. Of course you are my student but you have become more emotional and desirable."

I would experience pure joy at such times. I used to think that in his eyes I was a complete woman and that he would soon propose. Whenever we'd talk of marriage, he'd say—"Do you think that any marriage is a key to happiness?"

"Well, yes and no." I hardly knew about things then.

"There are no happy marriages in the world, Malvika. What seems beautiful today disappears tomorrow beacuse no woman is a complete woman."

"Really?" My diffidence loomed large and transparent.

"No, not in one physical being. A woman lives in bits and pieces in a myriad body, a patch-work of virtues and qualities which seldom make a whole, that's what I feel." His eyes were inviting and stirred a desire in me.

I was trying to understand, though I knew he was right. If no woman is complete, neither is any man. Not Bhupen, Dadaji—neither Papa nor Pierre. Their masculinity, the quality of being male, is the only truth about them. Mother is just a female—whether she is the beloved of Papa or a friend of Pierre—like Naina who eloquently demonstrated it by exploiting her physical charms to the hilt. Or be it Savita on the nuptial bed of Bhupen. The ultimate and sole truth about them was that they were women, a female body.

The train was transporting me to a past deeply cherished. Sharatji was engrossed in *Words* by Jean Paul Sartre. He got up suddenly and took out a glass and a bottle of Rum. No matter how much one tries, there are certain inescapable moments when the temptation to give into primary instincts becomes irresistible. More so, when one is drunk. It has been seen that in such a state, true nature along with all its crass shades, surfaces. Sharatji was reclining after having consumed half a bottle, facing the window. The dark sky outside flew across the window. The rest of the passengers had already occupied themselves with dinner. I continued analysing Sharatji's case history. He had fallen asleep and his face was looking distorted and warped. I put a blanket over him. He hadn't spoken a word all through the journey. I hardly knew him. I wondered why he had to drown himself to a stupor and become unconscious like that. One became so unpredictable in an inebriated state. Probably it was out of such circumstances that criminals were born. Whatever has once found root inside can never be totally forgotton—it is bound to emerge outside. I was disturbed by Sharatji for I had held him in high esteem. I was suddenly gifted by a keen insight. I don't know how—which made everything seem crystal clear. I realised that our experiences are not greatly different from what we anticipate of them.

***

I FELT A little unsure of myself when I set foot on the platform of New Delhi railway station. Although I consider myself to be independent and hardly lacking in self-confidence, a vague old fear crept up in me. Was it the effect of a big city, the weather or my loneliness? I couldn't fathom. The memories of the past once again took over and I was constantly thinking of Bhupen. It was strange, I thought. Colours do get faded with time, but they hardly ever disappear altogether, from a sensitive heart.

I had to stay back in Delhi after the Seminar to start with my questionnaires collecting data. Prof Sharat had introduced me to a research scholar. He accompanied me to the press. It was one o'clock by the time we had finished. He went away and I was again alone. Delhi was a city I had stayed in but I could hardly call it my own. Cities, I thought, can never be addressed thus, as your own.

My thoughts turned to Bhupen again. I was very immature to believe in Bhupen's attraction. It was my fault that I overestimated him. I had put him up on a pedestal from where he condescended to look upon me resplendent in his attractive personality and intellectual strength. Has any man been able to attain so much in one lifetime? Was it all there or were all these qualities merely a figment of my imagination? We perceive and evaluate to arrive at a judgement. This is truly awareness, but often we're overly hasty in making opinions about people. I got into a taxi and started for Bhupen's house. I remembered his house number and his rooms, small yet stylishly decorated, particularly that rack of his study where he neatly arranged all his books. Mostly they were biographies. Didn't one's choice of books talk volumes about one's personality?

"Which number?" The taxi driver queried. "E...." For a moment I was lost. "S-40," I told him finally. The streets of the colony looked unfamiliar. The houses were crowded together and there was no order. We had gone around twice when I got irritated. "Why don't we ask someone?"

"Okay, but it's next to impossible to pull aside away from this mad rush. It almost seems as if there's a big fire somewhere and everyone's off in a hurry to get there as fast as possible. The city is becoming crowded every day," the driver said.

We asked a shabbily dressed person who was carrying a baby in his arms. He indicated the house and we drove up ahead. I recognised the house immediately. There used to be a large tree and the house would recline in its shade. Today, there was just a skeleton shorn of foliage as if making mockery of all my erstwhile dreams. The man who had given us directions entered after me.

"Does Mr Bhupendra Mahajan stay here?"

"Yes," he stared hard at me, "Oh, its Malvika, what a pleasant surprise!" It was an indifferent welcome, negating and belying all former intimacy that had at one time existed between us. Bhupen had changed drastically, I thought. Had it taken a mere six-seven years to bring about a trasformation so complete, so radical…a metamorphosis? I was in a state of shock.

He indicated a chair and went in after opening the door. The sight of his disabled child filled me with a throbbing dismay. He stared at me with wide-open, stark eyes. I sank into an extremely dirty and run down chair, thoroughly disquietened. It was the same old story inside as well. The drawing room had an unkempt look about it—books, clothes and other things were strewn about. A pile of unwashed dishes added to the dismal air. The thick layer of dust hinted at the room not having been cleaned for a long time. Where were the books and the indoor plants which had made it so very pleasant and hospitable in the past? When I'd just love to come and gossip endlessly, gulping down barrels of tea. Why had Savita neglected her home so much? Was it out of frustration? Bhupen had returned. "Well, Well, how have you been keeping?"

"Oh, I'm well." It was all I could say.

"Mussoorie seems to have suited you. You look gorgeous."

"Maybe." I was too conscious of my ordinary looks and positively hated any exaggerated comment to the contrary. "What are you doing these days?" he asked.

"I am doing my PhD....after doing a Masters in psychology."

"How many years to go?"

"By January next, probably." It was brief and dry.

"What next?"

"Oh I'll try doing a psychoanalysts course. Let's see how it turns out."

"How's your mother? I'm sorry about your father's death. Somehow, I couldn't make it. It must have been very painful...."

"She's fine thank you. Busy running Nirmal Kunj. I teach at the convent. We manage our lives." I had no desire to talk about Papa.

A silence slowly descended upon us and settled down. The formalities were over. We kept sitting motionless, the fingers of quietude prodding and probing us for sometime.

"Have you written anything recently? One's quite cut off from everything in Mussoorie and one hardly gets to hear anything."

"No, those three novels were all that I could manage."

"Why?"

As if in an eloquent answer, his child came crawling out dragging one limb behind him. He was salivating and making strange incoherent sounds. It was distressing to be made so painfully aware of his incapacity. I could barely control myself from going over the edge and breaking down. It was overbearingly morbid. The dirty, dingy room was foul smelling and nauseating. Bhupen picked up the baby and took him inside. I could hear him speaking disconsolately to the child. It was all Savita's fault, I told myself. Bhupen came out with two mugs, the floating tea leaves in the tea appeared to me to be like dead flies. I sat back helplessly. Bhupen drank nonchalantly from his mug while I simply coundn't bring myself to touch it. I wanted to just get up and run away from this depressing situation.

"Savita isn't home?"

"No, she's gone for her duty at the hospital. She's working as a nurse."

"Oh!" I could barely manage to conceal my surprise. I was more than aware of her longing to lead a glamorous and prosperous life. She, Savita, reduced to being an ordinary nurse!

'Well, it's very simple to understand really. She had to do it for Anuj," he indicated the baby. "It's easier to get treatment at the hospital and all the facilities are free. There was hardly any other way we could manage it."

"I don't earn much and we have another child…a girl."

"When is she back usually?"

"I don't really know...it all depends on the duty roster. Sometimes she has to stay out all night."

"Have you stopped going to the college? I mean, have you given up your job?"

"No, actually the baby sitter for Anuj didn't turn up today so I had to stay back."

I objected…"Well, she could have taken leave too..."

He came back with simple logic. "She gets paid extra for a special duty like this one and besides I get paid for the leave. So it works out best this way."

What could I say after that? It is best to keep silent when ones beliefs and convictions have been recently shattered.

"The doctors say that he'll get well again. Maybe I'll be able to write again. I think that even our mutual disagreements have been largely due to the terrible strain we've been under..."

To me it appeared to be wishful thinking, much unlike the intellectual I had always believed him to be. It really became intolerable when the child started crying again. I got up. Bhupen went inside, wholly preoccupied with his disabled son. Good-byes were redundant and grossly unnecessary. Faith, love and trust exist within us as continual flows, not spontaneous isolated events. They live within us as the driving force—it's only that each ones perspective is diflferent. Why didn't I feel an empathy for Bhupen's child? Did I actually want to run away? He was so oblivious of things that I felt that I didn't even exist. The brilliance that had always shone in his eyes had somehow dulled. The spark that had attracted me to him and made me believe the conviction that by sheer dint of passionate zeal he would reach dizzying heights was no longer there. His academic pursuits would surely transform him from an ordinary mortal to the epitome of excellence. It was so utterly distressing to find him all disoriented and broken by circumstances too powerful for him. I simply could not identify the curious blend of anger, frustration, disenchantment and almost a sense of betrayal—he seemed positively ugly and revolting. Vaguely, I found myself in the bus, my head against the window pane, tears streaming down my face. A helpless rage filled me and I wanted to raze the whole world to the ground. Were only circumstances to be blamed for his downfall or the grave economic conditions?

***

THE DOOR OF Sharatji's room was open when I passed. He called out my name so I went in. He wanted to discuss the paper he was to read at the seminar. I took notes and tried to be relaxed and not sel-fconscious. I was quite used to drowning my frustration by throwing myself deep into work.

Work would invariably transform all my frustrations into a seething energy that could leave me drained of all emotions. I did not realize that the sun had set and it was dark.

In any psychological analysis, there is a subject and an object. I would get tired collecting data and conducting experiments. I could feel it even more so because of the state I was in. The tragedy of Bhupen's life was something that would take a long time for me to get over. The focal point of the most treasured of my memories had fallen apart, and it seemed like a tree bereft of all foliage.

"What's happened, Malvika? Are you feeling alright? You look very tired....."

I looked at him blankly, disoriented. Who is he?

"No, I'm all right...." I wanted him to take his hand away from my back, but somehow I couldn't bring myself to do it. There was something in me that was melting and thawing—a sensuous trembling. His hands were awakening something in my physical being and that night my body became my only reassurance that I was a woman.

When I woke up the next morning, the sun's rays were caressing my bare body. There was no hope or expectation on his face. He was sleeping next to me. His eyes looked serenely content. I remembered the desire in his eyes last night, that I had clung to, and that had made me more complete as a woman. Maybe I did not really want it to happen that way. Isn't there so much in life that happens without rhyme or reason? Whatever had happened had occurred without affection. His hand was not in mine and he turned away from me. It was almost as if he was a mere instrument in some cosmic design meant only to acquaint me with this truth—the truth of being a woman, maybe a complete woman.

While having a bath, I felt no different—as if nothing had happened. I wondered why people attached so much importance to quenching this dormant desire of the flesh. Bhupen's condition had definitely affected me much more. The pain of the soul outweighs those of the body.

***

THE NIRMAL KUNJ garden was in its customary full bloom and everything looked fresh and vibrant. This small hill station still lingered here from its colonial past. Cottages and walks still bore names such as 'Sir George'or 'Everest House,' 'Charleville Road,' 'Falcon's Nest,' etc. But over the years many other flavours had mingled to create a charming culture so characteristic of Mussoorie. Nirmal Kunj was also in itself a mixture of so many cultures. Its British architecture, mother's British mannerisms and along with that me, Bhaiji, typically Indian—simple and spritual Janaki depicting some kind of rural heritage, singing typical folk songs and speaking her own language. Whenever Roshanji came we had recitals of Mantras and performed all sorts of rituals Bhaiji had suggested. And now, we had Pierre who had his own language of pencil sketches, paints and oils. His creations were the signatures of his personality and his attitude towards India. I was stunned when I saw the piano. The old piano was saved from the clutches of Kishen Lal It was back at Nirmal Kunj and was placed in one corner of the Banquet Hall. It was made of original rosewood and had exquisite carving. Embedded in the carving were small brass shining nude figures which adorned various parts of the piano. The lacquer was perfect. It was a piece of perfection. Whenever I looked at it I imagined Pierre playing some kind of romantic melody on it and myself listening to it.

Bedi had told me about Naina's return. But sheer exhaustion kept me confined to my bed. It changed to fever—a fever that wilted my spirit and crippled my soul. I couldn't stop feeling amazed at how I managed to be so totally untouched by what had happened with Sharatji. My inner self was as chaste and unsoiled as before. The peace within was unbroken. Sometimes, I felt that the first embrace that I had cherished so much in my memory was so pure and pristine that it had made me impervious to everything else. The intensity of the feeling had sent me so deep within myself that any change was not possible.

Naina came to visit me one day. She had much to tell me about her concerts and her tours.

Suddenly I said, "Naina! you are looking gorgeous. It seems that the weather abroad has suited you well."

"Really! But I think it might have something to do with my being absolutely happy. That I could shake off all make-believe and be my own true self. It has been such a blissfully satisfying experience. Oh! I forgot to tell you something. The King of Nepal has promised to present me with gold anklets. He was enchanted with my performance and asked me what I wanted. I told him that it was traditional for dancers who perform gracefully to be given gold anklets."

"How wonderful!"

Pierre entered just then. I introduced them to each other. At first they were formal with each other and Pierre offered to show her around the house. I had thought that when Pierre met Naina something unexpected would happen. They returned after she had seen his paintings and sat by me—Pierre had some tea sent for.

"Many of your landscapes portray the farmer and his plough. Is it because you have taken a liking to our countryside?" asked Naina.

"No, the plough is a symbol of man's triumph over nature. The act of digging the earth fills the farmer with an overwhelming masculine confidence that nothing is unsurmountable. He can conquer anything he desires—even a woman's body."

"Pierre, you mean to say that a woman is only a body to be trampled or crushed. What about her intellect, her ability to rise above a normal being?"

"You are so right, Naina," Pierre said. "Today's woman is definitely more than a mere body. She only gets trampled if she desires it, not otherwise."

He continued, "But there are times when the body is all that matters. I think a woman can be defined as a being who makes a man feel that he is a man, and if it does, it is her supreme achievement."

"You are so wrong. It is a woman's understanding that matters. Submission of the body has no meaning if she is not an understanding person."

"Malvika, you have no experience. The body too has a language which means it can only be tackled by a body. A woman's body," continued Naina, "should be so explicit that the listener should become speechless, and the spectator or a listener totally stunned. That was my achievement over the years."

"You are contradicting yourself, Naina. A few minutes ago you told me that you felt happiest while you performed. Your art gave you perfection which you never possessed earlier, though your body always existed with its colourful rainbows."

"I am not a thinker like you Malvika, I cannot put into words so many things I feel. But I must tell you that the body is definitely an overpowering entity. Sometimes its sensuousness drives you crazy."

"I feel happiness is largely a matter of finding ones life

work in the right direction of knowledge."

"No, it's not so," Pierre said. "If it was so, why would women spend so much time fixing their hair, attending to their makeup. Most women spend a lot of money on cosmetics, perfumes, oils, etc. Why? Isn't it to attract men towards their physical charm and not to their intellect."

"I think men are to be blamed for it Pierre. When you men talk of a woman, you mainly talk about her physical charm rather than her intellectual achievements. Besides that, art has made the modern man sex conscious. Art and the commercial exploitation of a woman's body down to her last curve has made men more conscious of her physical attributes.

"The best thing is that women have submitted themselves to this commercial exploitation."

Just then Mother came to fetch Pierre.

"Aren't we going out for a walk?"

"Hello aunty! How are you?"

"I told you not to call me aunty. You call me Vibha, or Vinnie. Anyway I am fine, how are you?"

Ma's face had become red with anger while her fingers were continuously fixing her new coiffure.

"I am fine, Mrs Nanda."

"Excuse me, Naina, I must go for my evening walk. I am glad I met you."

Pierre slipped out of the room.

***

NAINA AND I went to see a play *Kunti—The Human Voice*. It was a bilingual production, something that had been evolved from Shankar Pillai's *Kunti* and Jean Eocteau's *The Human Voice*. Kunti, a character from Mahabharta had been given special powers by God. She could summon any Devta at will by the use of a special hymn. After she had cohabited with Surya, the Sun God, Varuna the God of air, Yama the God of death and Indra, the God of water, she gave birth to Karan. It was indeed surprising how such an independent woman could be callous enough about her illegitimate child to abandon him. Karan was floated down a river and was thus forced to live a life of virtual ignominy, deprived of the glory that was rightfully his.

I started wondering about the relevance of Kunti's character in today's world. The woman of today bears children and runs a household without questioning her lot, virtually like a beast of burden. She spends her whole life in the shadow of her man. Maybe the portrayal of Kunti today is necessary to awaken and inspire today's woman. Do women like Kunti actually exist—independent and in complete control of the circumstances around them? Kunti raises herself from the level of the rest of the characters in the epic Mahabharata and actually builds up a world of her own. When we try defining or describing a complete woman, we fail miserably. Kunti is radically different from

Gandhari, another character in the epic. She is neither sedate nor satiated like Gandhari. On one hand, she allows herself the pleasures of the flesh, and on the other, she feels the guilt of being an unwed mother. The same Kunti tricks Karan later into parting with his impregnable armour to save the lives of her five legitimate sons. She is extremely inspiring as a mother and her life is full of ups and downs.

The play depicted the time when Kunti and Gandhari are renouncing their kingdoms after the war. Kunti is nostalgic for a moment and a trifle guilty about having indirectly caused her own son Karan's death by taking away his armour from him. She also remembers the time when, prior to her marriage, she had invoked the Sun God to enter her body by the use of a sacred hymn.

Naina and I were quite impressed by the play, especially the dialogues. "Is it relevant to portray such characters in today's plays?" asked Naina.

I replied, "I think it's become imperative that people should understand that women are not the weaklings that they have always been believed to be. There is a Kunti in each one of us—bold and independent enough to take decisions and even ready to make sacrifices for the children. Don't you know that all of us women are in the cosmic perspective, precious and rare."

"Malvika, I never knew you were so spirited. I do hope some of this enthusiasm rubs off on me !"

"Then I must accept Pierre's proposal!" I continued rather impulsively.

"What are you referring to?"

"He told me that he paints best on a woman's body. Especially on the breasts—their contours provide a mountainous landscape!" I told her.

Naina was not scandalized at all. "That sounds interesting. You were right—there is a Kunti in each one of us, ever ready to be adventurous and daring."

It was quite cold by the time I reached Nirmal Kunj. A heavy silence hung around. It gets dark so abruptly and early in the hills that one longs to see the sun go down slowly and disappear. I really missed the long lethargic evenings which could be so full of possibilities. The door to Mother's room was ajar. As I tiptoed quietly up to my room along the corridor, I couldn't help looking inside. Mother and Pierre were on the gigantic bed, totally nude. It was a tender sight. It was for the first time that I realised how beautiful Mother was. Was Pierre making the painting on her nude body, the one that he wanted to make on mine? And I had put him off at that time. I didn't feel bad at all. It didn't seem to be a transgression or repulsive to me. I realised that bodies had a beauty of their own and in love the charm was manifested many times. It was somehow divine. Was it equally divine between Dadaji and Johar Bai? Was I in the wrong about all this? Was it the immediate effect of the play that I had just seen?

Naina had confided in me one day…"Can't you see that Pierre is very attracted to your Mother? Now do you accept that a woman's body is her greatest weapon, to win a man's attention and seduce him?"

It seemed to me as if I was being confronted with a profound truth. Naina had said it easily and effortlessly. I had till then avoided acknowledging this possibility, which had become common knowledge. How long could I keep it under wraps of my heart's ignorance?

"Hey! I hope I have not said something very personal," Naina almost shook me to get me out of my reverie.

"No, not at all. I think I sensed it but refused to even admit it to myself. What is going to be the eventual outcome of such an association, Naina?"

"Very simple, I guess. To me, it's either marriage or the physical part of the relationship that takes care of such associations."

"Do you think it's proper for Mother at this age to indulge herself"

"Proper, indeed! Look, we all have our own definition of propriety and we act according to our own concept of morality." Naina had uncanny logic.

"But at this age?"

"Malvika, love has no boundaries. Love is a fundamental need for us and if we don't love then it means that we are not at peace with ourselves."

I couldn't help saying... "Even widows have a right to live...."

"Not merely a right to live, but to live according to their whims and fancies," Naina completed if for me.

"What do you think I should do about it?"

"Try to keep your Mother happy. She really needs it."

"I must think about it."

"No, don't think too much. The more you think, the more complicated things will seem. You will be totally biased by your past experiences, by all those factors which have gone into your making. You must be an observer of whatever comes to pass. Your Mother is a woman too, who cannot live without a man. One who is used to having bread with butter can hardly do with mere dry bread."

Naina tried her best to convince me. I was offended. "What nonsense! How can you say such things?" It was very strange for me to understand the definition of this kind of woman.

"This is the truth that you have shielded yourself from. Probably because your traditions and your culture make it impossible for you to see what is so obvious. Malvika, the time has come that we need to know the needs of our species. We deserve a citizenry with minds wide awake to know how the modern world is progressing."

"Maybe you are right. I feel it all deep inside me but

somehow, I find myself unable to express it. Something within me dulls the process of thought and compels me to be silent."

"I think you are being unfair to yourself. You must not let anything suppress you so. You must let the real 'you' emerge. Oh yes, here are some books that I had borrowed from your library. This is a wonderful book on Indian dances. Johar Bai must have been a scholarly woman. It is such an intensive study on classical dances."

"We will talk about it some other time. Why don't you go and keep the book back yourself?"

"Okay then...be seeing you....."

I kept wondering about Mother. Did the memories of Papa mean nothing to her? How could she forget all the love that had existed between them? I could never imagine forgetting Bhupen and that was hardly a relationship. Did I mean nothing to Mother? Was I merely an obstacle in her way, an encumberance to be gotten rid of? For her and Pierre? The example of Johar Bai was clear before my eyes—she had given up all she had to be Dadaji's mistress, incurring the wrath of the society, to belong to him alone.

It was an ordinary morning full of routine. We were at breakfast and Janaki was in the kitchen singing as she made us stuffed parathas. Ever since Kishen Lal had left Nirmal Kunj, Janaki had been singing religious songs, mainly related to Radha and Krishan. The one she sang now went like this:

"Aana sunder sham hamare ghar aana,
Aap bhi aana, Radha ji ko bhi lana."

(Oh Shyam Sunder, please do come to my house, do come to bestow your blessings, come with Radha, your divine lover).

The bhajans she chose to sing were laced with universal love and relationships rather than religious fervour.

"Didi, here is your paratha. Why are you always so quiet and lost in thought? Memsahib you never speak to her like a mother. You two behave as if you are not even related. Sometimes I wonder…Memsahib, tell me, is she your step-daughter?"

"Will you shut up Janaki." I shouted at her. "Go inside and get on with your work."

Pierre was enjoying his stuffed parathas. I wanted another but Janaki did not show up for long. I went to look for her in the kitchen and found her missing from there too. What a strange woman! Just then, I saw her returning to the kitchen. She was holding an empty plate in her hand.

"Where were you? I want another paratha."

"What can I do…that Swami had two parathas and tea. He wants some more. Shall I give him another?"

"Who is this beggar?" Ma was very angry.

"Ma, all Swamis are not beggars," I corrected her.

"He has come to meet the French babu."

"Who is he?" asked Pierre.

" The same Swami Roshan you met at the shrine. He has brought you something."

We looked for him in the verandah and lobby. Where could he have gone? Bedi came and informed us that he was in the library. We found him perched on the library stool. He was taking books off the top shelf. Those books were Johar Bai's collection.

'These are Johar Bai's books. Why do you want to read them? Please don't touch them." He looked embarrassed and instantly put down the books.

"I am sorry I came to the library without your permission. In fact, these books are my…Anyway, forget it, see what I have brought for you," He brought forth a three foot high statue made of alabaster.

"This was created by an Italian artist but look at the theme, it's so Indian. A mother and child."

"What a beauty! Who is the artist?"

"I wouldn't know the name."

"Where did you find it?"

"I have always seen it in my house. It used to be in my mother's bedroom. But I left home many years ago. Someone from home brought a lot of things to the mandir. This was among them. I thought of gifting it to you. I have no idea about these material goods. All I know is that this is a work of art. You people appreciate and understand the value of art so I brought it for you."

"Who was interested in art, your mother or your father?"

"I wouldn't know. But there were a large number of artefacts in our house."

"Can you get me some more?"

"Nirmal Kunj is full of things, why do you want more? Can I borrow these books?"

"Of course you can, but don't leave so soon. Rest for a while."

"Yes, do stay back. I like talking with you," Pierre said.

"Do that and I will bring you a paratha."

"All right, Janaki…Ma."

"You know Janaki?"

"Yes, he has been coming here often to borrow books." Janaki commented.

"How did you know about this vast collection of books?" I was trying to reach the potential and reality of Roshan.

"Come on Pierre, we have to go to the Sachdev's for lunch."

Mother interrupted our conversation midway, as she entered the room. "Oh, he hasn't yet left!" She pointedly aimed this last remark at Roshan.

"Just look Vinnie, he has brought this beautiful statue for me. Isn't it out of this world?"

" Good Heavens! This statue is from Bhaiji's house in Dehradun. How did you get it? Are you one of those antique dealers? Have you bought this or stolen it from there?"

I noticed that Roshan could control his temper in a fraction of a second, without anyone being the wiser. He replied quite calmly. There was a magical power in his boldness.

"I don't know what you are talking about. This is mine… in fact it belongs to my mother. My father gifted it to her when I was born. I am not a thief. I am gifting it to this gentleman because he will value it more than I do." He picked up the books and went away without waiting for our reaction.

"Vinnie, you could have been more charitable to him. He is an intelligent and a sensitive man. He does not seem to be an ordinary sanyasi. He has renounced this world at such an early age and seems to have risen above materialistic things. Besides, he has gifted this priceless statue to me. A thief cannot gift anything."

"Perhaps you are not aware of the fact that in India it is these swamis and yogis who indulge in all sorts of nefarious activities from drug trafficking to theft."

"Ma, How can you make such sweeping statements? Surely every Indian is not characterless."

I couldn't restrain my anger. Suddenly, she softened and asked Pierre to move.

"Come, let's go from here. Everyone knows the store was full of antiques. Janaki has been selling them over the years."

"Really ! I wasn't aware of that—where was I?"

"You were busy with your school and your studies.

Besides, they were broken and useless articles."

"But you should not have permitted this if you knew about it. Besides, being valuable they all have a story to narrate. They are a part of our past...a part of our family history, the collection of my grandfather."

"Why do you always attach so much importance to antiques. Why do you always enjoy wallowing in the past? Sometimes I feel you are as crazy as Bhaiji. Come Pierre, we must move. You know I like to be punctual, specially at parties."

Watching them go, I realised that they made a handsome couple.

***

JANAKI HAD NOT reported for work for the past four days. I had been missing her. Her magic touch kept Nirmal Kunj spic and span. Janaki was just like a bad habit that once inculcated was difficult to get rid of. Ma hated people who ate in any other place besides the dining table. But Janaki knew that I loved to sprawl on the floor in the library and nibble on tit bits, with my cup of coffee. The best part was that Janaki never let mother know that she spoilt me with her loving indulgence. I felt lost without her.

I went to her room and found her sitting in a corner in a very peculiar manner. She looked absolutely different. Her face was distorted and colourless like bleached cloth. She looked pale and weak. I had never seen her like this. She was always vibrant and bubbling with life, singing all the time, filling the atmosphere of the Haveli with life and freshness. She was dressed in a soiled saree. It was a strange sight for a person who was always neatly dressed. I was very sure that something terrible had happened. She looked at me with her pale eyes as if I was a stranger. "What's happened Janaki? What has happened to you? Speak up. Why are you sitting like this?" I touched her softly.

She collapsed in my arms like a felled tree. "Why don't you tell me? How can I help you, please tell me. Are you unwell?"

Janaki, who was always laughing and singing, started to cry.

'Tell me, has Kishen Lal come here? I am sure he has been here. He is the root cause of the trouble."

"No...No." She started crying more loudly.

"Should I call a doctor, if you're feeling unwell."

"I have been to the doctor, but even he could not save…"

Her sobs became louder.

"Save whom?"

"My child."

'Why didn't you tell me? You could have talked to my mother. We could have taken you to a good doctor."

"Bedi brought a midwife," she continued to cry.

"I have never cried till now Didi. I never gave in to all the inhuman cruelties he inflicted upon me. This Kishnwa married me when I had barely stepped into my teens. Soon after a year, he said that he was going to divorce me since I had not borne him a child," she said.

"Do you know Didi, he tried to sell me off in Delhi for five thousand rupees. It is my good fate that I somehow managed to escape and find my way back to Nirmal Kunj. My father has never questioned my decision to stay on here in his quarters, although he must have suspected something. Kishnwa keeps visiting us here but I am not going to go with him ever. He has always taunted me for being barren. And now when this infecundity showed the sprouts of fertility he was nowhere around to care for it. How will I ever be able to show him my face. It's not easy to bear children when you are in your late forties." She started to cry all over again.

I tried to pacify her but she seemed disturbed to the core of her heart. She could not seem to hear what I was trying to tell her. I sent Bedi to fetch an ambulance. I took her to the hospital, arranged for the best medical aid and she recovered from the trauma and the shock in a few days. While she was recuperating, I would often ask her to sing a song, but she would ask, "What should I sing? It is neither Phagun nor Savan, rather it is cold weather, a time when you go into hibernation, just before the metamorphosis."

I could see Kunti's face getting submerged with Janaki's.

***

ONE DAY, MA asked me, "Malvika don't you feel attracted to Pierre?"

I just laughed. How does one define 'attraction'. My

relationship with Pierre was like it was with any other guest who came to Nirmal Kunj. These relationships were not sentimental and were quite meaningless for me. Only once, just once, I had been impulsive enough to consider submitting to Pierre's overtures.

In the process, I had stumbled upon another truth that the body was sometimes more powerful than knowledge. But this was so only for people who had the cunning to use it—for me, it remained only an instrument of my survival—not my identity.

Mother said, "I do not know why, but I like him Malvika. I am attracted towards Pierre. Do you think my feelings are normal? I don't know but I feel complete when he is around; is it a sin to love someone at this age?"

"Do not worry Ma, every natural feeling is normal, even this attraction of yours. I think you are lucky to be gifted with love all over again in life…accept it gracefully."

"Are you sure, Malvika? What will society say?"

"What society? A group of faceless people. Where were they when Papa died and the two of us were left alone to fend for ourselves in this world? We had no money, no roof over our heads. Where did all your friends go…those who decorated your social evenings and kept you away from reality, the reality of your own existence."

"But what about your Uncle?"

"Bhaiji is sensible. He will understand…."

"Malvika, I had never imagined this possibility would ever crop up in my life. It just happened, and I cannot help it."

"Ma, just listen to what your conscience suggests to you, your heart is ultimately your true friend."

"There is no bigger enemy either."

"If it was not an enemy, how could it be a friend?"

"Malvika, will you be able to forgive me?"

"I am so happy for you, I always wish you happiness. I feel so great today, specially because you have confided in me like a friend. Don't worry about me, Ma. Go and decide things with Pierre and I will go to Dehradun to meet Bhaiji."

Ma looked happy. She hugged me, and I could feel the warmth in her embrace. Her eyes were glistening with happiness as they always had when Papa was alive. I could hear Janaki singing a funny kind of folk song.

"Mohe naye gaune ka chav
Naina lade nandoi se"

(I want to remarry as I am falling in love with my brother-in-law)

Janaki was slowly returning to her normal self.

***

I DON'T KNOW why my journey reminded me of Bhupen and his unmatched ability to recite Rabindra Sangeet. Pierre and I both sat quietly in the hired taxi. I thought how simply nature always stood before me, and with what fond and familiar ease it filled my heart with freshness while with

Pierre I felt an unfamiliar kind of tugging, as if the currents were drifting us apart. It was the month of March, and on the plain lands of Dehradun, the mustard cultivation was in full bloom. The rough road was uncomfortable and reminded me of the 'Song of the Bamboo', that Bhupen had once recited.

'O South wind, the wanderer, come and rock me; Rouse me into the rapture of new leaves. I am the wayside bamboo tree, waiting for your breath to tingle life into my branches. O Southwind, the wanderer, my dwelling is at the end of the lane. I know your wayfaring and the language of your footsteps. Your least touch thrills me out of my slumber, your whisper gleans my secrets."

This was the first time I was ever visiting Bhaiji or the city of Dehradun. And this was also out of necessity for the strange kind of responsibility that I shouldered. Pierre had a sketch book in his hand and had made some abstract pencil sketches. Why, I wondered because he always made sketches of human faces or the various objects around him. I wanted to break the silence.

"Pierre, let me see what you have sketched so far?"

"Nothing much. The surroundings are not inspiring enough."

"The mustard fields and the wild bamboo groves are quite colourful."

"Sometimes, even colours cannot arouse any kind of feelings and pencil sketches don't relate to the colours of life. Rather, they are the naked truth of one's innermost or hidden feelings."

There was a jerk. We had reached Bhaiji's house. It was a simple small house with a garden. As Pierre and I entered the living room the first thing we both noticed was an identical white marble statue that Roshan had gifted to Pierre. Pierre touched the statue without giving away his familiarity with it. Bhaiji said, "Pierre do you like this statue? My father gifted it to my mother the day I was born. It has been here at this very spot, on this marble pedestal, since that day."

"It is very beautiful." I wondered why Pierre did not mention anything about the identical statue that he had received from Roshan. We talked about various things not daring to pick up the strands of the topic we had come to discuss. I was aware that Bhaiji and Mother had never been on the best of terms. Bhaiji was barely cordial to her and Mother never accorded him the respect that he deserved as head of the extended family. He often used to comment,

"Your mother is not bothered about the values and traditions of our culture. Her modern outlook is very ambiguous. I find her personality weak and pitiable. I always find her strange."

After dinner, when Pierre retired to his room, I was left alone with Bhaiji. I made some coffee for him and for myself and sat next to him in the comfort of his large diwan.

"I have to tell you something."

"What?"

"It is about Ma and her future. Ma and Pierre are in love with each other. Will it not be proper that they should get married? Of course with your blessings."

"What trash is this?" He was obviously shocked beyond all his expectations. I knew it was too much for a traditionalist like Bhaiji to swallow.

"It is true Bhaiji." There was a long lingering silence between us.

"I had heard about it vaguely, but I did not want to believe it. Has she actually told you that she wants to get married to Pierre?"

"Yes, I have had a talk with her, but we have not discussed the marriage. I wanted your consent. In any case, Pierre wanted to visit you."

"Just imagine. This is really Kalyug—the dark ages—when a daughter talks about her mother's wedding. Bitto, your mother was always like this. I always knew that she would come up with something scandalous. That is why I brought her to Nirmal Kunj—to keep her away from Munna's friends, and Delhi life. Only, I did not know that one cannot interfere with destiny."

I wanted to say something but I knew it would be meaningless.

The next morning when Bhaiji encountered Pierre, he did not waste any time.

"You wish to marry Vibha, our bahurani?"

Bhaiji's expression was so stern that even Pierre felt uncomfortable.

"Yes, why not, if she wants to."

"What about, Bitto...will you treat her as a daughter?"

"What do you mean Bhaiji, I will not be Pierre's daughter. We are friends, and we shall remain friends. I have my own identity. It has nothing to do with my mother. Why should I get involved in their relationship?" I did not like Bhaiji's conversation.

"You are right, perhaps it's better to remain friends." Quickly he walked away towards his room. I knew he was upset. Maybe there were tears in his eyes.

On our return to Nirmal Kunj, there was a letter informing me that my thesis had been approved and that I had been granted a Doctorate. I told mother about Bhaiji's consent and of my result. She looked very happy, and for the first time she hugged me and kissed me on my forehead. I was touched by her rare intimacy. We all wanted to celebrate—everyone for their own reasons. Pierre opened a bottle of champagne. Mother sipped champagne from his glass shyly and they kissed each other. The only person who looked indifferent was Janaki. Her silence was obvious and deliberate and effective enough to disturb our happiness.

Pierre wanted to get married in France, in a small church which was located in his native village near Paris. They both started planning the forthcoming wedding and I could see that Ma was very excited, like a teenager. She had always wanted to visit Europe. All her dreams were coming true. She was going to live in Paris, the Paradise of high fashion and design. There are only two horrifying mishaps in life—when you cannot get what you desire the most and secondly, when you suddenly achieve all that you have ever wanted in life. Everything seemed hazy to me, as if it were not actually occurring but was a pencil sketch with suggestions of formations. But pencil sketches cannot depict the truth clearly or correctly. There was no reason to be suspicious of Pierre. He had stayed long enough with us for me to trust him. But I believed in well-defined shapes and colours of reality. I wanted Pierre and Ma to be married here. I wanted to be sure. Ma was hesitant and not entirely in agreement with me. In the end, it was decided that we would go to our temple, where to my satisfaction, a simple Indian wedding would be performed.

We started preparing for the journey. Bedi was full of enthusiasm but Janaki was extremely quiet. I was keen to hear her opinion on the situation, as I always felt that she had a mystical insight into life. She always had earthy solutions to social or personal problems. Her simple carefree attitude to life was reflected in her choice of folk songs. She was intelligent in her own way.

This time, the journey did not appear as tough as it had

been the first time. Ma was also quiet. She was probably engrossed in her future plans, full of new possibilities... or at least the hopes of new possibilities. Pierre was quite relaxed. He was busy taking photographs and making pencil sketches. I wanted to be away from them, to absorb the whole situation. The space would provide me with enough grounds to get over my anxieties. As I walked on that muddy road following the erased footsteps of the past, I wondered what grandfather, grandmother, Bhaiji and even Johar Bai had felt when they chose this path. What had brought them here—the attraction of the darshan of the deity or their own inner conflicts? One steps out of the comfort of routine, to undertake a hard journey of pilgrimage only when one is convinced that it is unavoidable. Only those who have the insight, the ability and the courage, are able to rise above the mainstream of life, an act which leaves them totally isolated. To be banished has always been considered the most unbearable of all punishments. I remembered the patients in mental hospitals whom I used to visit during the course of my research. They would wait for Saturdays when they were visited by their relatives. They even started waiting for me, for their sense of isolation was very painful. Suddenly, I thought of Roshan, living all by himself in surroundings that were far removed from the hard realities of the world. Maybe he thought that by coming to terms with his violation and the sorrow in this life, he could achieve complete detachment in this world and happiness in the next.

Pierre stood in front of me. He had picked up some wild roses. He handed a few to Mother and said, "Here love, the time has come for me to gift you flowers. I will try to weave a wreath of happiness around you. Will you put this wreath of fresh flowers around your neck, and in your hair?"

Ma blushed like a teenager. He turned towards me and gave me the rest of the wilderness he had gathered.

"To you for being a good friend, Malvika. Your claim on me is more than that of others, maybe that is why you are always so silent."

"Thanks, I will always be proud of you, Pierre." I wanted to walk away from Ma and him, but he persisted and said, "May I ask you a question Malvika?"

'Yes."

"Why don't you change?"

"But why? What is wrong with me?"

"I think you are too serious for your age and you have a recklessness in your nature which makes you different from the crowd…you stand apart."

"She doesn't even smile or laugh like other young girls. She has no desire to dress up or even to look smart. I don't know why she is like that. Sometimes I wonder whether I gave birth to her? We two are so different," Mother also commented.

"Is it because you lost your father so early, Malvika? Is it because of your financial difficulties?" Pierre wanted to probe.

"No," I did not want to commit myself, but I had to give some definite answer.

"Pierre, I think I, as a physical being, am not disturbed by physical pains or financial losses. They don't touch me. What I do feel all the time is that there is an unquenched thirst within me to know, to really know about everything, maybe the universe, or my existence, perhaps your existence in my life or maybe Roshan's renunciation of the world. I am so full of curiosity to know the truth which I think will help me attain the ultimate Truth. Most people don't impress me because they are unhappy, miserable, jealous, envious, and even anxious and so in a state of total confusion."

"But the Universe or Nature is in total order…it is no confusion."

"Maybe, but the order of the universe is not my worry. I know what is within me, and I know what I am searching for."

"What do you think of relationships? They don't matter to you, your mother, Bhaiji or maybe Roshan."

"Relationships are like your pencil sketches, which are not definite. They can be wiped off or they can be emphasised in a way that can change their shape. They can even be coloured by adding emotions to them, to become landscapes. You are creating a painting out of them—your marriage, your future life full of activities will be a definite painting. A portrait of joy."

"Why can't you create a painting like that? Marriage is a very natural happening. You should get married too."

"I don't know, Pierre, I don't feel the urge to. I feel I am complete...I have the courage to see things as they are...I do not need experiences."

"Are you happy in this mental state Malvika?"

"Yes, I am, because when I look at something, I don't see it as it really is, but the way it should be. I feel a strange bond and become one with that object and the situation. When this happens I feel everything else is inconsequential. There is nothing outside, everything exists within me. This unique feeling, this oneness gives me a completeness, the meaning of 'the real me'."

"I don't understand what you say."

"Okay, forget it, forget me, and enjoy your wedding day. Let me go and look for Roshan."

I could not find Roshan anywhere outside the temple. The whole place was so quiet and solemn. I wondered how and where Roshan lived. Had he reached the stage of self fulfilment, where he did not need anything else to make him feel complete? As I reached the innermost chamber of the temple, I spotted the reassuring flicker of a tiny earthen lamp. Roshan was sitting on a torn piece of carpet. His eyes were closed, probably in deep meditation. He looked very pale and vulnerable. He projected the kind of vulnerability that makes you feel instantly protective for no apparent reason.

His meditation was interrupted by my entry. When he opened his eyes and saw me, there was a strange kind of glitter in them. Strangely enough, his eyes reminded me of Bhupen. Bhupen when he kissed me. Yes, there was no difference between that physical reality and this awareness.

"Malvika, how come you are here?"

"Sorry for disturbing you. I am really sorry...I should not have entered here like this."

His voice sounded like a soothing invocation to God as he spoke, "Don't worry, there is no need to say sorry and there is no restriction against entering any chamber of the temple. There is no inside, outside or any other dimension here. There is only one awareness which flows and I know you are very much a part of it. Have you come alone Malvika?"

"No, Ma and Pierre are also here." Just then Ma entered the temple.

"Come in, *maaji.*" Roshan welcomed them but the word *maaji* was not liked by Ma. Her face contorted with a controlled anger. Pierre and she sat in front of the deity and I sat next to Roshan.

"You have to perform a wedding," I told Roshan.

"Who is getting married?"

"Mother and Pierre." The word "Mother" echoed in the hollow dome of the inner chamber of the temple. How meaningless it appeared!

"But I don't have the slightest idea how to perform any ritual, leave aside a marriage ceremony. I am not a professional pandit, Malvika. I just live here in this place because it provides me with favourable surroundings to achieve a certain kind of fulfilment. I am a seeker and my search is on. I am here to study and gain knowledge. I am not familiar with worldly affairs, least of all a wedding ceremony."

"See Malvika, didn't I tell you? I never wanted all this fuss." Ma's face was full of confusion.

"Do not worry Ma," I tried to console her, "Swamiji, let us just pray that the two of them live happily together. Please bless them, so that my mother's new life may be a happy one without even a faint image of her old misfortunes."

Roshan looked at me for a long moment. His gaze was so intent that I looked away in confusion. He got up to pick a book from the bookshelf and started to recite some mantras. His voice was powerful and his narration was very melodious. But I was more engrossed in the wedding rather than the meaning of the mantras. I put Ma's right hand in Pierre's and placed a few flowers in their palms. I helped Pierre to put the red 'Sindoor' in the parting of my mother's hair and on her forehead. Roshan handed some more flowers to me and to Bedi, and we all jointly blessed Pierre and Mother by showering flowers on them. Roshan even gave some sweets to me to be given to the bride and groom. Then he turned towards me and said,

"What an unusual situation for me to perform a wedding and that also where a daughter is giving away her mother in marriage, that too to a foreigner."

Then he turned to them. "With God as witness, I declare you husband and wife." Pierre held mother's hand and said, "Vinnie is my wife. We shall share everything as long as we live. I will take care of her."

It was a very joyous moment. Roshan even picked up the 'Shankh' (large sea shell) and blew into it to declare that the ceremony was over. This strange foreigner had gained today what I had lost, I thought. I turned around and found Ma crying. I wondered why she was shedding tears? She was the gainer, she had so much new to achieve. It was I who had lost a mother, but I had no desire to cry, so I told Pierre in jest, "Look your wife is crying. What kind of a husband are you? Look after her, she is all yours now."

I left them to themselves and to the solitude they deserved. Roshan also followed me. I reached the platform where we had enjoyed coffee when we had first visited this place. Relationships had changed and a strange feeling of loneliness overpowered me. I felt like an orphan and from somewhere Kunti's face started haunting me. My mother is a woman first, a multi-faceted woman, and not only a mother. Is it not sufficient to make a woman aware that her relevance is in keeping her womanhood alive?

"What are you thinking?"

"Oh, Swamiji."

"I have explained to you so many times, Malvika, that I am not a swami, I have not renounced the world. You can call me Roshan."

"It is a strange name, Swami Roshan or Swami Roshan maharaj, or....."

"No, don't add adjectives to what I am. Let me be what I am in total reality of my own self."

"Why did you decide to live here?"

"Well, when I was a child I used to come here with my mother. She never used to go inside the temple, she always used to sit here on this platform and pray. We came here whenever I had holidays or on my birthdays. When I grew up I went inside the temple but my mother still waited outside and I realized she was a Muslim. She lived in Musoorie but I went to Dehradun, and completed my schooling at Doon School. Sometimes, I resented her coming here, but she said because her husband was a Hindu and his family believed in this God, so this place was a place of worship for her."

"Did you ever ask her about your father?"

"No, I was always in such awe of her that I could never ask questions. Besides, her love was limitless and formless, and was too great for any petty questions."

Lost in the memories of his past, he continued, "After School I joined college in Dehradun. Once, when I came home in the holidays, my mother was not there. She had just disappeared without informing anybody. I was so shocked that I never went back to college. I looked for her everywhere. I thought she would be here, in this temple, as she was very fond of this place. She was not even here, but I decided to wait, and continued to wait. The old Sanyasi who used to live here adopted me and treated me like a son. The people around revolted against his gesture. They commented on my doubtful origins. They felt the temple would be polluted because my mother was a Muslim. That is why very few people come here. But Guruji was above all this. He believed only in the individual and the soul....He was above physical and perceptual limitations of ones body. He used to quote Kabir,

'Never ask the caste of a Sadhu' (*Jaat na poocho Sadhu ki*). My Guru educated me. Till then, my knowledge had been limited. The more I learnt from Guruji, the more I discovered my ignorance. He made me rise to a higher level of observation through his teachings. I discovered that religion was only a limitation in the progress of an individual. Our purpose in life is to discover and rediscover our own inner self which is limitless. It is only this awareness which matters. No religion in the world can provide us with this awareness. It has to come to us from within ourselves. One has to discover for oneself to attain the fullness that is joy or *Ananda*."

A long quiet moment stood between us. We sat

spellbound like two statues.

"Did you try to find out who your father was?" I knew my question was meaningless for both of us.

"No, because I knew that there are certain truths, just as there are some names, that need no introduction."

"If you knew everything you should have gone back to your father rather than come here."

"A father is supposed to accept his son, to give him an identity. Surely my father must have felt some kind of constraint that made him justified in not accepting me. Personally I did not want anything from him. There was no need—my mother had provided me with a complete life. She gave me so much love that I do not need anymore even for the future."

"Where is she?"

"Somewhere in Calcutta. She is unwell. I have been thinking of visiting her."

'Will you let me come along?"

"Of course I will. But why do you want to."

"It has been my lifetime's desire to meet Johar Bai."

"How did you know she was my mother, who told you about this—Janaki?"

"No, there was no need to make any kind of inquiry. The truth cannot be hidden—it is always there for us to understand."

***

SO THEY WERE married, and they occupied Johar Bai's bedroom in Nirmal Kunj and lived like husband and wife. It was an awkward situation for me, but I had to adjust. Till now my attitude towards the whole affair had been uncontaminated by any negative thoughts, but suddenly I felt there were some blurred boundaries between Mother and me. She did not like me calling her Ma anymore. Sometimes, she even objected to my long conversations with Pierre. I enjoyed her suspicious wifehood. But I wanted to avoid division. All that was happening to the environment was acceptable to me, it was becoming a part of me. I wanted to remember her as she was to me, not as related to Pierre or anyone else.

For every child 'Ma' is a psychological sense of security. Maybe this security is the reason for clinging to ones mother. I thought I knew myself, but I really did not. I was also changing, moving, as I used my education and learning for my own satisfaction. This fragmentation reminded me of *Kunti* the play I saw with Naina. The multi-faceted Kunti, a princess who had supernatural powers to make love to any Devta she desired, which she made full use of. All her life she enjoyed the motherhood of five powerful Pandavas as well as the respect bequeathed to a Queen Mother. While Karan, her illegitimate son suffered the misinterpretation of his identity all his life. Kunti gave birth to him and even became the cause of his death. A mother cheated one son for the sake of her other sons whom she wanted to save from destruction. Kunti fascinated me as a powerful woman of unique character.

Pierre was in and out of Mussoorie. He was busy preparing a new passport and visa for mother. They were to decide the date for their departure. Janaki and Mother were busy packing up things for her. I also made her pack all her sarees and jewellery. We even packed some old paintings which Pierre admired. Mother did tell me a couple of times, "Malvika, keep something for yourself, some jewellery and sarees, what will I do with all this?"

"Oh, you will wear them. You look beautiful in them—for me they are meaningless."

That evening, Ma and Pierre were away to Delhi and I was alone in Nirmal Kunj. I had sent Bedi to find out about Naina. I wanted to tell Naina about my mother's marriage and wanted to share my feelings with someone. But she was not there. Mandira was also not there. I sat alone near the reception desk where mother usually sat. Suddenly I saw Sharatji walking in, and I felt very guilty that I had not gone to meet him after my result. I immediately received him with warmth and happiness.

"I am so happy to see you, Sharatji."

"So am I."

"First you must forgive me for not visiting you after my results were announced."

"Yes, I was wondering, what had happened to you, so I came. Congratulations, you deserved it, and I must say, the examiners have given excellent comments on your thesis. I hope you know that they have recommended the department to publish it."

"I am so grateful to you for all your valuable support."

"No, you yourself are so hard working. Where is your mother, Malvika?"

"She has gone to Delhi with Pierre."

"Pierre…who Pierre......Oh, that French painter you introduced to me on New Year's Eve?"

"Yes... Pierre has married my mother and very shortly they will be leaving for Paris."

"What....that's sensational news. When did this happen?"

"Last month."

"What have you decided about your future?"

'Well, I will join college. I have already applied for the Lecturer's post which was announced recently."

"That will be nice. Maybe one day you will reach the position I have retired from."

"What, have you retired?"

"Yes, I am free like a bird."

"What will you do now?"

"Go back to my village, to the family, or may be somewhere else."

"Wherever you go, do something creative. Maybe

you can write a book. You are so good with the human personality! You have prepared so many papers on the subject. Compile them and do write a book. You don't need it but if you want I can help you."

"You have always been so supportive and helpful, full of positive ideas, that is why I admire you."

"Oh thanks."

Bedi announced dinner and Sharatji stayed back. We both had a very simple quiet dinner. He talked about his village, the complexities of his life with his wife and his son. I knew his passionate melancholy was beyond repair. But I managed to convince him to give it a try. When we parted, I knew he was convinced enough to attempt to create a genuine future for himself. It was going to be a present, because he had always believed in Destiny and waited for a miracle to happen.

***

AFTER ANY UPHEAVAL in life, there are countless possibilities for organising oneself all over again. I, too, wanted to reorganise my new situation of solitude consciously and dispassionately. Before Ma's departure I organized a simple dinner for the few people we knew in Mussoorie. It was a sort of an announcement to society. Janaki had suggested it to me. She had always been worldly wise, and understood human society more than Ma or me.

Naina came an hour before the party. I was thrilled to see

her. We talked about Ma's marriage and she congratulated me for what I had done.

"Hey, I am so proud of you Malvika, you did the right thing."

"What is my contribution in the whole thing? It was more of a sort of non-interference in Ma's and Pierre's life."

"That's not true! I believe it was a temple marriage, and you were the witness. Malvika, tell me how many daughters have the heart to go through that. Instead of getting married to him yourself, you got your mother married to him."

"No Naina, you are wrong. I never wanted to get married to anyone; Pierre was never my kind of person. I enjoyed his companionship because he was intelligent and humane. He has achieved some kind of awareness because of his art. Anyway, tell me where were you all these days? I was looking for you. I wanted you to come to the temple for the wedding."

"You will be surprised to hear where I was."

"Where were you?"

"I have gone back home, I have gone back to Naresh and to the mother-in-law who bitched at me all my life. Sometimes, miracles do happen....Yes. Once I was performing on stage...the proceeds of my performance were to go to cancer patients and I felt that performance of mine was one of my best, Malvika. I remember that once Guruji told me that whenever one performs with selflessness, it is like a prayer to God. The experience was unique. I felt something was happening to me…as if my whole physical being had evaporated and I had disappeared. It was very strange, but I experienced it."

"You know something, you tasted the state of pure consciousness, which is so rare."

"How can a person like me who is drenched in all sorts of sins on earth experience a pureness of being?"

"No, I am sure whatever you did was what your circumstances demanded. Somewhere your 'Atman' remained untouched and pure. Your dedication to classical dance took you near perfection and near God. That is why your consciousness made you experience spirituality the way you did."

"Anyway, after that moving experience, when I came out of the hall I met my mother-in-law. She was sitting in the car waiting for me to come out. She somehow managed to take me to her home and there I met Naresh who was suffering from various ailments. He reminded me of my son. I cried, he cried, and all of us just sat together. I don't know whether it was right or wrong, but I compromised because of Mandira. I want Mandira to have a name, a father, a home and a definite future to help her to lead a secure life unlike mine."

"This is fantastic. I am so happy for you Naina and for Mandira."

Bhaiji entered at that moment. Pierre and Ma also came down to the Banquet Hall where we had arranged the party. Suddenly it reminded me of a birthday party which Papa had arranged for me. What are these parties for, to celebrate what? Maybe people do celebrate to get over the boredom of being alone. Ma tried to wish Bhaiji but he ignored her. Naina came to the rescue. She started talking to Ma about her future plans and what she would do in Paris. To my surprise, I heard that she was contemplating opening a beauty parlour or going into fashion designing.

Bhaiji noted down Pierre's address. His conversation was pointedly querying. He wanted Pierre to correspond with him. Pierre came to Sharatji. "Sharatji, why you are so silent?"

"Oh no, I was just thinking."

"Thinking about us?"

"Oh no, I was thinking about happiness and its duration. It comes like rain and disappears like a bubble, or may be like a cigarette which goes up in smoke! We make so many compromises to achieve that happiness, particularly with our thinking and beliefs."

"Happiness is always on the surface, it is never deep. One is constantly searching for it. Maybe I will find it in my togetherness with Vinnie," Pierre answered.

"But Sharatji, if one does not desire happiness, one does not have to compromise." I was still on the same wavelength.

"No Malvika, life is neither happiness nor any compromise. It is a research. The kind of research you did to achieve your Doctorate. And during that research happiness can only be felt."

"Okay, let us dance," and Pierre took Naina to the floor.

Davidji had repaired the old piano and there was an orchestra for the first time in the Banquet Hall since we had come to stay in Nirmal Kunj. I enjoyed the music. It was some old number. I did not know much about music, but I could see Pierre, Ma, Naina, Sharatji and other guests enjoying it. Ma looked very happy. In between, Janaki came in to serve something or the other and I felt there were many mixed feelings in her expressive eyes.

The day Pierre and Ma were to leave for Delhi to go to Paris, I felt uneasy inspite of all my inner strength. Bhaiji did not come out of his room to wish them good bye. He remained inside his room, silent and withdrawn. Pierre, Ma and I got into one taxi, and when we were about to leave, Kishen Lal's harsh voice came through the darkness.

"So, the bird is off on its flight as I knew she would. After all, this Haveli has Johar Bai's blessings. Love and lust flow in this Haveli like wine and water One has to drink it."

It was useless to comment or argue for there was no time for such things. I held Ma's trembling hand in mine and discussed various travel arrangements and the number of items of her luggage. The flight was early next morning, so we had decided to travel late at night. We started after dinner, and fortunately reached Delhi by five o'clock in the morning. We drove straight to the airport. We washed and changed in the cloakroom and had breakfast at the coffee shop. Soon, it was time for their departure. Mother hugged me and repeatedly said, "Forgive me if you can Malvika."

"Do not feel guilty, Ma. You have done no wrong. You have found yourself a companion, a friend to live with. I appreciate your choice, he is a fine person and will take care of you. I am sure you will be happy. Besides, I am not a child. I am mature enough to look after myself. I am not alone, Janaki is here and I have my job and Nirmal Kunj and above all, Bhaiji."

Pierre also hugged me. His eyes were tender with affection.

"Malvika, I must convey my feelings to you before I leave your country. You are great and your country is super. Living with you in Nirmal Kunj was a rewarding experience. I appreciate the human aspect in your relationships. The way Janaki is looked after in your household; Roshan has been placed on a respectful pedestal and people like Naina are cared for—it is all very remarkable. I felt very much at home and it was all because of you, Malvika. Today, I feel as if I am leaving my own home and my own family behind. I was touched by the way you got involved in our wedding. Anyway, 'thank you' is a very small word for all that you helped me to experience and cherish in this wonderland called India. Don't worry about your mother, I will look after her...come to us whenever you feel like...I will wait for you...Okay, Malvika."

"Yes, you must come soon Malvika." Mother had tears in her eyes.

"Yes, I will. Ma enjoy yourself. I will pray for your happiness."

The announcement for the departure of the Air-France flight appeared on the television screens.

"Okay Ma, bye Pierre. Look after yourself."

Soon they were lost in the crowd. My eyes were wet but within myself I was stable, quietly praying for Ma's future. When I turned my face towards the Exit gate of the airport, I suddenly felt there was a crowd, a stream of people around me, but I was alone. I would have to be alone and utterly independent in the future. I started moving slowly towards the gate, towards a new kind of freedom, freedom from Ma, who never loved me, and freedom from the guilt that I was her daughter. As I was stepping out of the gate, he was coming in with a wheelchair with a distorted human body seated in it.

"Oh, hello Bhupen."

"It's you, Malvika, what are you doing here, at the airport?"

"Well, I think the airport is a very interesting place…

you greet new faces and bid good-bye to your loved ones. It is a place where you receive or you lose something."

"Malvika, you are just the same, as enchanting and beautiful as ever. Well, I am about to leave for London. My flight is a few hours late. I decided to wait here as it was not possible for me to go home and come back with him. How about you?"

"Ma has just left for Paris, I came to see her off'."

"Why haven't you gone with her?"

"She has married a French artist."

"Oh really!" I could see his expression. "What will you do now?"

'Well, whatever I did, it was without her. If one has to do something, one has to do it alone. Anyway, I have finished my research."

"Oh good, so you are Doctor now. Doctor Malvika. I was sure you would achieve something worthwhile. You always possessed a very sharp and probing intellect."

"How about you, Bhupen?"

" I don't know what happened to me, Malvika, I don't know how my life became so startling and strange—should we sit somewhere, if you are not in a hurry? I want to talk to you—in fact I wanted to talk to you the day you visited us, but suddenly you disappeared."

We both moved towards the coffee shop. With a lot of care and tenderness, he settled his invalid son on the wheelchair and sat next to me. I wanted to feel close to him and experience the old warmth. I hoped it would arouse some kind of sensuousness but surprisingly I felt nothing. There were no vibrations at all and my inner emotions— my heart—was quiet, stagnant and still.

We ordered coffee.

"So Malvika, I am so happy I met you, before it was too late. I wanted to share some of my private convictions with you, maybe because I still feel the old proximity to you."

"I am also keen to know, why and how things happened?"

"Let me start at the very beginning. Malvika, I don't know how Savita created a fragment of a rainbow, which I had envisioned for myself. Anyway, I was happy when we married. She was happy till we discovered we were not meant for each other. There was no compatibility between us. Maybe, she had no potential to hold me, my sensitivity or my interests. There were indisputably subtle differences in our approach to the physical chemistry of love. Life became an examination with each of us trying to cram our spellings and learn the grammar of love. Then came our two children, one after the other. Our daughter was normal but Anuj was born like this. We both tried, we tried hard to work out a solution, to help each other and carry on. But we parted. She decided to take our daughter with her and I was left with Anuj, whom I love too much…maybe because I feel he is truly symbolic of what happens to a humanbeing if his emotions are crushed in an unsuccessful marriage. Savita, in all those years, damaged and crushed my self-confidence with her persistent nagging and impulsive behaviour. With my son, I retreated into a sad and sullen silence."

I gazed at the expression of sadness that was too deep for his large eyes. How I had adored those eyes. Bhupen had been a progressive creative writer, but this surrender to his love became his downfall, leaving him in a situation where he was helpless and withdrawn.

"I know Malvika, I was aware of the affection you had for me, but I could not reciprocate it, because Savita's physical attraction was too alluring. Maybe this was destined, it was to happen, and you also never asked for anything."

"Well, my emotions were too immature at that time. It was more of an infatuation. I feel that if you admire someone you are not supposed to ask for anything. Admiration or even love means only giving. Give whatever you can, don't ask. And the miracle is that when you give out of love it is returned a thousand fold, and all around you, flowers start to bloom.One cannot imagine what happens, unless one experiences it. I don't know why I said all that."

"Have you started writing poetry Malvika?"

"No," I laughed, "Why do you think so?"

"Because you philosophise about everything, and your expression is like a reflection in a mirror—clear and visible."

"Anyway, it was a pleasant coincidence that I met you.

I shall pray for Anuj's quick recovery. I must take leave as I have to get back to Mussoorie."

"Malvika, thank you for sparing some time for me. Let us hope we meet again."

'Yes, come to Nirmal Kunj, whenever you want. It will provide you with the perfect ambiance to write."

"Let us hope so."

***

THE CITY OF Calcutta fascinated me as we got down at Howrah Railway station, which was full of all the variety of life a city can provide to its visitors. There were human forms sitting, waiting, eating or cooking food or just sleeping on that dusty platform. For me, it was a mysterious land of art and culture. The birthplace of Rabindra Nath Tagore and Rabindra Sangeet. Outside the station was Howrah Bridge, a massive structure of iron carrying the onus of routine life in buses, cars, taxis, bullock carts, etc, on the other side of the Hoogly River.

Victoria Memorial stood majestically flanked by many palatial buildings reminding me of the British rule and our colonial complexes. I had expected to see Calcutta with lots of large gardens, flowers, manicured lawns and beautifully kept bungalows. Instead, it was a jungle of dirty multi-storeyed buildings, which were extremely ill-maintained. Roshan and I sat in a taxi, very close to each other, but he was lost in his own thoughts and I was restless within my own. I felt sorry for the landscape of Calcutta.

"Roshan, don't you feel that the shadow of British India is still alive here? Calcutta portrays a certain kind of humiliation that the colonial rulers had forced on us."

'Yes, I also feel strongly against the British. They were the people who crushed the real character of Hinduism and true *Atman* of Indians. Maybe because their psychology of Raj was based on hypocrisy. All those people who came to India to rule actually had a selfish motive. They enjoyed India like a retreat and enjoyed the slavery of Indians. What they liked most here was the humbleness and faithfulness of Indians, specially the uneducated group who served them. These domestic servants put them on a pedestal like God. The attitude probably originated in our scriptures that tell us that a guest is as venerable as God (*Atithi Devo Bhava*). They changed our educational pattern, introduced convents and Christianity. I am sure they knew that our spiritual and religious studies, and holy books like Vedas and Upnishads were supreme and would transport us to infinite heights of spirituality. They discouraged Sanskrit and Vedantic studies in schools. English as the main language was introduced, and it gradually overpowered our thinking, and we became what we are today. We neither reached the true heights of Christianity nor did we remain true Indians."

"Don't you think, Roshan, they shook our self-confidence too, beyond repair, and left us in a state of self-criticism where we despair about ourselves and our future."

"Yes, and since then, we have lived a life of contradictions. On one hand there is so much wealth in the country and on the other hand there is hunger, filth, disease and beggars. So many riches, yet so much of starvation. Don't you feel, Malvika, your mother was a perfect product of that kind of contradiction and that is why she married Pierre; otherwise who could have had the courage to do so?"

"Maybe you are right. Anyway, I am happy for her. She was so restless in Nirmal Kunj. Mussoorie was not her kind of place."

"And how about you? Do you like the kind of life you are leading there?"

"I don't know, but when I analyse my situation, I am not unhappy either. I have never attached much importance to the place because I am not a very sociable being. I am not so fond of people, friends or parties. So Mussoorie, and Nirmal Kunj have become my treasure trove of learning about life, Nature and above all, myself."

"Malvika, you surprise me. Why aren't you like other people, worldly and empty-headed like your mother, or Janaki? What prevents you from changing yourself?"

"Why should I change?"

"Because you have never asked yourself that question".

"Roshan, can I ask you the same question, will you be able to answer it?"

"Malvika, there has never been anyone in my life to ask me any question, leave aside this one. And you know that I have never attached any importance to myself. I think there always has to be an external catalyst which makes you undergo a change. It can be anything—a person, circumstances, environment or maybe even God."

"Will you change now? Can I be your external catalyst?"

"I don't know, first let me meet my mother."

"Oh yes."

"You know something, Malvika, you resemble my mother so much in your mannerisms and speech. When I first saw you, I was stunned at the strange similarity."

"You think so."

"You know I don't talk of illusions."

We had entered an old residential area of Calcutta. On one side were palatial houses which were surrounded by new buildings and blocks of flats. The whole area had a featureless character. The sky was immense and the whole horizon was far away. Our taxi stopped near a building that had a big white rusted tin sheet painted with faded letters 'Nav Neer' which was the name of the Senior Citizen Home where Johar Bai lived. We both got down. I paid the taxi fare and with our sparse luggage we entered the main gate.

The whole building seemed to be an old gloomy bungalow. The walls were unpainted and dilapidated. The structure of the house was heading towards decay. We crossed the lawn, which had a big tree in the centre with a few old ladies sitting under it. They were withdrawn and quiet, apparently enjoying the shade. None of them bothered to ask us anything, so we entered the main building and reached a verandah, from where we could hear the strains of a Bhajan. We followed the melodious notes of the Bhajan and soon found ourselves in a big hall. On a big durrie was a small congregation of women, sitting and listening to a young girl who was singing with a Tanpura in her hand. Most of the women were engrossed in the music and the ones who looked at us, all had eyes with some kind of shadow of the past which reminded me of Bhupen. Why did Rabindra Sangeet always make me feel sad? I looked around searching for Johar Bai, a long lost face which looked like mine. Almost all the women wore a forlorn look. They wore simple sarees draped in the Bengali style.

When the music session ended, all of them stood up. Some needed help while getting up, and others limpingly helped themselves. We stood up and wished them with folded hands. Some of them blessed us with a smile, some came near us to touch our heads. One graceful lady, who seemed to be the manager of the institution came towards us and asked, "What can I do for you?"

"We have come from Mussoorie. Are you Jaishree Ji?"

"Yes, I am Jaishree."

"I got a letter from you. My mother Johar Bai lives here

and she is sick. Can I see her?"

Jaishree's face clouded with anxiety. She was a middle aged woman with an impressive personality. She looked at Roshan's white sanyasi like clothes unbelievingly. How could Johar Bai's son be a sanyasi?

Jaishree looked at me and asked, "And you?"

"I am also related to her; tell us where is she, we are desperate to meet her."

She was again silent, then she spoke hesitantly.

"She died last night. We have already sent a telegram, and this Bhajan sabha is a sort of condolence meeting for her."

"Oh, no." Tears filled my eyes. I must have been trembling because Roshan helped me from falling.

Jaishree said, "Please come with me, we were infact waiting for you."

We both followed her. Roshan's grip tightened on my arm but he was very quiet, while Jaishree spoke of Johar Bai's life in 'Nav Neer'.

"Oh she was a great woman. She, infact, was the one who helped me build this old age home. She managed everything. She took part in all the activities, helped women to be creative in some field or the other and utilize their time fruitfully. She sang every morning and sometimes danced for them. It is a home with a difference. Women live here like a family, and she was the life of the Home. Didn't you notice how many women were weeping during the Bhajan service?"

We reached the room where Johar Bai's body had been laid to rest. Her body was wrapped in a white sheet. A small earthen lamp burnt near her head. We sat close to her body. Roshan removed the sheet from her face. It was an old face but without any wrinkles. She looked so peaceful, as if she had just fallen asleep. Roshan put his hand on her forehead. I am sure he must have prayed just as I did. I am sure at such moments, investigation and logic all vanish and we become weak. Roshan closed his eyes, and I felt intensely for him. How much I had wanted to meet Johar Bai, and to talk to her. She had always been my mysterious goal, and now that I had achieved it she was dead and gone.

"We do not have much time, we have to take a decision. How should we perform her last rites? By the Hindu custom or by the Muslim?" Jayshree broke the silence.

"You knew she was a Muslim?"

"Oh yes, she had not kept her life a secret. She told us everything—how she started her life as a dancing woman, a *tawaif* with a masters degree in music and how she had fallen in love, and became a devoted wife to your father. She would often remember you Roshan and would write regularly to you. Were you receiving the letters?"

'Yes I was. She was my torch bearer, my Guru, who taught me to rise above this meaningless and empty world."

"Why did you not visit you mother earlier?"

"She never permitted me."

"Everyone loved her here in 'Nav-Neer' and respected her. She was a close friend of each one of them. She also spoke Bangla fluently. Not only that, she recited shlokas and mantras every morning at the prayer meeting with an unusual grace. She observed all Hindu festivals and fasts, but she also prayed and performed namaz five times everyday. She had such an extraordinary personality. She was a real scholar. She knew four languages; she was the one who taught so many women to be literate and created an unusually big library here. She was the most precious pearl of our string." Even Jaishree could not control her tears.

Roshan continued to recite mantras for sometime. While he did so, his right hand constantly touched Johar Bai's forehead. After a while he got up and said, "I will go and make arrangements for her burial. Yes, we will bury her. She was a Muslim, lived like a Muslim, so her last journey must be what she truly was."

Everything was over; a part of Malvika was also to be buried along with Johar Bai. This sorrow, what we ordinarily call feeling, is a different stream, different from the stream of my imagination. It is a sorrow, much deeper—sorrow of thought, self-pity or the sorrow of the image? But I have to get out of this state.

***

A HUMAN BEING is basically a 'wanting' creature. I also wanted completeness. All my compelling desires were expressing themselves in this human sense of want. Janaki was going to provide me with a certain kind of completeness. For me, Janaki's pregnancy was a source of joy and wonder. A new life was finding a way between darkness and light, and was demanding freedom.

"Isn't it amazing, Roshanji. The five elements are going to take a human shape," I whispered.

Roshan was not at all as excited as I was.

"Five elements are not so important Malvika, they are not as glorious as the soul is. It is the soul within that small body that is refusing to remain imprisoned in Janaki's womb."

"What is freedom?"

'To be in the body in a physical sense but to be above all physical expressions."

"What is that state?"

"I will explain it to you when you have the time."

Time, really, was a rare commodity—taking care of middle-aged, pregnant Janaki, Nirmal Kunj and my lecturarship in the college. I was on the move all the time. Janaki was very weak and it was a difficult delivery. A healthy baby boy was born and Roshan named him Manu. With the help of a nurse and Bedi, I helped Janaki and Manu come out of danger and they recovered. Manu was a pleasure and filled up Nirmal Kunj with a new excitement. He reminded me of a new efficacious wave whenever I saw him. Janaki was no more in the annexe of the house. She shifted into one of the rooms of Nirmal Kunj, very close to my room.

One day, I found Kishen Lal in Janaki's room. He was sitting on a chair comfortably with a beedi in his hand. I was furious. He was not allowed to enter Nirmal Kunj.

"Who allowed you to enter this room? And how dare you smoke next to the baby."

"Who can stop me? This is my wife and my son, I don't need anybody's permission."

"If you were so fond of being a father, you should have come earlier. All these years you thought I was a barren woman. You humiliated me, brought all sorts of women here to prove that I was not a complete woman. I used to feel inadequate and almost ashamed of myself. But now—now my Manu has proved to me that I am not less of a woman than any other, and today for the first time, I am neither weak in front of you as I used to be nor afraid of you." Janaki looked different as she said all this. Her face glowed with her new motherhood and confidence. In a swift courageous move, she got up and pulled Kishen Lal by his right arm.

"Kishen Lal you get out of my room. I will not tolerate your presence in my room even for a minute. You get out of here. I don't want to see your face, our relationship is over, I don't belong to you anymore."

"Janaki sit down, don't talk loudly, it is not good for your health." I handed her a glass of water.

"All that she needs is to be hit with a shoe. She enjoys being slapped." Kishen Lal slapped Janaki in my presence. I was shocked at his cowardly behaviour.

"I am your husband. I am your master, woman and you are suppossed to obey me." He tried to hit Janaki again. But this time Janaki stood up like Kali Ma, dark and glowing. She wielded a wooden stick which was used for the baby's mosquito net, and started to hit him as hard as she could.

"Had enough of your nonsense. I suffered enough of your torture, my husband, now you get out of my life, otherwise I will kill you. I don't want your foul shadow on my son. Didiji please take the baby away."

I was stunned by her sudden strength and courage. Her transformation bewildered me. I picked up the baby and shouted for Bedi. I was perplexed at the ugly turn the situation had taken.

"Hey...leave my baby here."

Kishen Lal tried to snatch the baby from my arms.

"Why should I?" I also screamed

"Didiji don't let him touch my child. I want to keep him away from this horrible man. I want him to grow up into a normal human being, not an animal like he is. Besides Didiji, Kishen Lal has run away from jail, do something Bittoo Didi, save my child."

"What can she do your Didiji, she herself has no position of respect. The whole town is spitting on her face.

She has seduced a poor swami with her youth. She lives in this Nirmal Kunj with Roshan without marrying him, like Johar Bai did. I am at least married to you." His laughter was poisonous and filthy and vibrated through the mansion.

Bedi and the nurse freed Janaki and me from Kishen Lal's clutches. We called the police. Within a couple of hours, Kishen Lal was taken into custody. He went away but he left behind the stench of his misdeeds. Janaki fell ill as a consequence of all that excitement and agony. Manu was also affected and would cry very often but nothing happened to me. I continued to be normal. Sometimes, I liked Manu's crying as it was an announcement of newness in Nirmal Kunj; sometimes I hated it as it reminded me of Kishen Lal's cruelty and ugliness. For some inexplicable reason, I started disliking Manu. I could not disassociate Kishen Lal from his existence.

It was another cold evening and Mussoorie had a heavy snowfall. Nirmal Kunj was very quiet without any guests. I was sitting alone in my room when Janaki brought in the baby. His loud wails engulfed the frozen day. I closed my eyes and recited the Gaytri Mantra. Janaki stood quietly for sometime, then placed Manu near my feet and went out of the room silently. As I opened my eyes, Manu was not crying any more; on the contrary he smiled sweetly and I instantly cheered up. I picked him up in my arms and I thanked God for not making Manu a handicapped child like

Bhupen's Anuj. 'God' I thought, 'we keep forgetting what all we have'. I kissed Manu's forehead and decided I would always maintain my equilibrium regardless of the situation—successful, unsuccessful, conducive or non-conducive.

***

WHENEVER I LOOKED at the grandeur and magnificence of the mountains against the blue sky, it affected my heart. I felt as if the glory of the mountains had taken me over. It absorbed me, and temporarily washed off all my worries and problems. Roshan's presence in Nirmal Kunj was also as important and he was there as a pillar of faith and strength. Because of him, I did not miss Ma or Pierre, though their rooms always reminded me of them. Some of Pierre's pencil sketches were framed and were hung on various walls of Nirmal Kunj. They kept his memory alive. Very seldom did I receive letters from Pierre or Ma. The letters were mostly coloured postcards carrying few lines which conveyed their well being, rather than carrying any warmth of relationship. So they were meaningless and mechanical, without any value of a memory.

When I heard that Roshan Ji was preparing to return to the shrine, I was again disturbed and overwhelmed by sorrow. Sorrow of a loss which I had never felt till now, not even when Ma or Pierre left Nirmal Kunj. I had all sorts of thoughts which brought conflict and pain. Parting from Roshan was going to cause me a certain kind of fragmentation. I wondered why I felt like that. Was I seeking some kind of security in Roshan?

"Why do you want to go back to the temple?" I asked him. He did not answer. I provoked him as I definitely wanted an answer.

"What are you going to prove by living like that? What? You are neither a writer nor a sanyasi. Isn't your place in the temple improper?"

"Is it proper for me to live here…with you…in Nirmal Kunj—what is my position or status here?"

"Well, Nirmal Kunj is yours. Now when I am aware of the past, and know who you are, how can I allow you to go?"

"Malvika, decisions taken without any rational thinking are invariably proved wrong."

"Where is the scope of thinking. It is a decision that you will not go, you will not leave Nirmal Kunj till I am alive."

Unconsciously, I took his hand in my trembling fingers. Suddenly, I don't know why, I felt weak, and physically also I needed him, his security. He put his arms around my shoulders for the first time. His touch soothed all my conflicts and tensions. It had a magical mellifluousness.

"But what will I do here Malvika?"

"Don't you think it will be a good idea if we convert Nirmal Kunj into an old people's home just like 'Nav-Neer'. Old, helpless, homeless and lonely people could come and live here like a family. You could take care of them. And along with it start teaching Vedanta—our society needs it."

"Is this a repentance?"

"No, my decisions are never a result of any repentance. I believe in one's inner truth. I feel anything one does should be based on that truth. That is the only way to live up to certain standards."

Roshan took over the new project. Niraml Kunj was divided into two parts, one half remained a guest house and the other half became the 'Sewa-Ashram'. We had ten old people living with us. Each one had a past, an interesting past which became their painful present. Roshan, with his high degree of clarity and sympathy, helped everyone become aware of the vital significance of relationships which was the cause of their confusion. He used to meet each of their problems like a challenge and attempt to resolve it. Roshan was returning to this human world gradually. He had a network of roles to play for different people; for some he was a brother, to others a son, or a guru. He tried to help everyone to untie their knots, or enbalmed their bleeding wounds with his kind nature. He did not believe in any set outline or objective. For him, his function was more important than any status. In fact, we all lived like a family, and it was this creative process which brought about a beautiful change. Our living in Nirmal Kunj was not mere living. It was an art of relationship which our group learnt from Roshan who never had any relatives, or from me who never believed in any relationships. The process of living together was in the spirit of an enquiry, and then came the achievement of a clear awareness of a common purpose which helped and strengthened each individual and the group as a whole.

Bhaiji visited us very often. He never commented on anything or complained about Roshan's presence in Nirmal Kunj. He was well aware of the rumours regarding Roshan's relationship with me. I am sure he knew, as truth is very transparent and vibrant. Besides, he loved me and had faith in my character. I am sure he knew about his identity. In front of Roshan I felt I was a wave born a minute ago and soon destined to die. For me, I was not water, I was born of the sea, which sustained me and unto which I would return.

Naina came to Mussoorie with a dancing group to perform some kind of ballet. She wrote to say that she would be staying at Nirmal Kunj with her troop. I was thrilled. After a very long time, Naina walked in. There had been an immense silence of time between the two of us. But there transpired the most exquisite experience of life. When Naina came that afternoon, I was playing with Manu. We were playing hide and seek in the garden. Nalna watched us play and then happily hugged me and said, "When was he born? What a lovely child? Why didn't you inform me about his birth?"

"He is Janaki's son."

"Isn't she too old to bear children, I don't believe you."

"If you believe in me and in my vision, then it is true that Manu is Janaki's gift to me and to Nirmal Kunj."

"And what are you upto? Living on fresh air and water?"

"At the moment I am enjoying the fruits of our garden. Just look at these trees, they are so bountiful in their blossom. Come and have a bite of this luscious plum."

"Do not eat so much Malvika. It's not good for your health."

"Then what is good for my health?"

"A regular life, a home, a husband and children of your own."

"Naina, is that what you believe in? You, who all your life suffered because you married Naresh? Is this the nectar of all the experiences you gained in your lifetime?"

"Malvika, you have always been my 'confession box.' I confessed everything to you...my sufferings and my happiness. Maybe I have come all the way to tell you that I am happy now, happy in the true sense. I have rediscovered my long lost happiness in my art. I have forgiven Naresh for the untold misery and unhappiness he caused me. Naresh begged my forgiveness and wanted me to return to him. But tell me Malvika, how can I go back to a man for whom I have no respect, the very basis of a sound marriage? I have become resilient to all the pain life had to offer. Mandira has also grown up into a beautiful and confident young lady. She helps me in my dance school, she has a career and a loving mother which provides her with security and a bright future.

"You are great to be able to forgive and forget all that was so painful. I am so happy for you."

"How is aunty, I mean your mother. Any news?"

"She is very well. She has done a beautician's course and is going to open a beauty parlour of her own."

"Good, it is so satisfying to know that all is well."

Suddenly Janaki came with a glass of milk for Manu. Manu neither wanted to drink milk nor go to Janaki.

"Take him in Janaki, haven't you recognised Naina?"

"Oh it's Naina. Didi, my eyesight is weak, and I am growing old. Besides, she has also come after a long time."

"Janaki, congratulations for having Manu, at least you have someone of your own." Naina got up with a jerk, which was so typical of her demeanour.

"No, Didi ji, Manu is not mine he does not belong to me…he is Bittoo Didi's child. She is everything to him, whatever you call it—a mother, a master, everything."

"I am so glad Janaki, I hope you are well?"

"Everyone who lives in Nirmal Kunj is very well Naina Didi. This place is full of people who had problems and no relatives. Nirmal Kunj has become a real home for them. Our Bittoo Didi is like a window, and everyone can see through this window, the infinite sky and the sunrise and sunset, birds and flowers opening and releasing their fragrance."

Janaki would have continued but she had to leave as Manu wanted to go in.

"Janaki, will you ask Bedi to make coffee for us?"

"Malvika, I am so proud of you, you have done so much for humanity. You always thought of others, what about you, your own future?"

"What is so doubtful about my future? Life is full of so many things and I have concentrated all my energies and my passion on developing a peaceful life for my people in Nirmal Kunj. All of them possess a lonely, aching soul. They are all tired and helpless. I want them to live, to live a complete life and feel secure in these walls, walls which could not provide security to Johar Bai or to Roshan." Janaki brought us two cups of coffee. "Here, drink your coffee, you must be tired. I am so happy to see you Naina."

"And I am missing aunty so much. If she had been here she would have scolded me for my bad manners."

Naina had settled down in the huge garden chair with her feet tucked in.

"Malvika, I forgot to ask you something important—the gossip going around about you, I suppose you are aware of it?"

"Why don't you say what you have to, clearly."

"Well, who is Roshan? What is his relevance in your life? How is he related to you?"

"You know that I don't believe in relationships, Naina. They are meaningless for me. I am very fond of him because he is the only complete human being I have come across in my life."

"Are you emotionally involved?"

"I don't know how to define emotions, but there is no question of a physical relationship. Basically, I feel we are the two banks of the same river, our origin is the same. We are together, under one roof, and we have one aim in life—is that not sufficient?"

"No, it is not."

"Well then, let me tell you, when I am close to him I feel I am close to the infinite sky."

"Marriage is the only complementary institution. If you love him, why don't you marry him?"

"How can you talk like this, as if I don't know marriage is not complementary. It is an institution I don't believe in. I have no faith in it. The real meaning of togetherness is to live an organised life, with a complete wisdom. Love is always unconditional tremendous sensitivity to beauty, a great revolution, which we both are trying to bring about in our Nirmal Kunj."

"What about sex and love, Malvika—how can you deny the body and ignore its physical needs? Does it have no meaning for you?"

"As far as I know Naina, love is only a feeling. It is so personal, and one can mould sex to such a refinement that it becomes love—it has nothing to do with physical arousal or satiation."

"Do you think it has nothing to do with physical attraction? Then why does one maintain ones body, wear revealing clothes, or stay well groomed to attract the opposite sex?"

"I remember Naina, that you once said that man uses love as a weapon and treats a woman's body as a battlefield. He always likes to be a winner, a warrior who has won a battle. He maintains his women for his own satisfaction, not out of love."

"May I tell you a very amazing fact Malvika? Most men have no capacity to help their women to reach an orgasm. My experience is that women reach it only when they are in the right kind of mental state. Orgasm has nothing to do with the physical contact of the two, it is mainly mental or psychological. I am sure if man had that capacity, he would never indulge in rape. I am sure it is the total understanding of the situation which leads to a state of real pleasure, that is the first step towards the journey for truth."

***

NAINA TOLD ME she was going to perform a ballet in a small village called Lakhmandal which the people of

Mussoori were not aware of, though it was very near it. Lakhmandal had an interesting historical background. It was the legendary place where Duryodhan, the eldest son of the Kaurava clan had plotted to kill the Pandavas by burning them alive in a palace of wax. Merging the incidents of history with classical dance, at a natural authentic venue was a unique experiment in itself. She told me she had already performed at Khajuraho and at some other temples of Mathura and Vrindavan. In the series of those performances this one was the last. She wanted me to go with her to Lakhmandal and I agreed to accompany her. While we were discussing the plans and were preparing to go, I received a letter. It was from Pierre.

'Malvika,

Every painting has a background against which characters are placed and developed and given a form. Every situation has a significant theme. Trees also cannot be separated from nature just as light cannot be separated from the Sun. If one tries to separate them, the division destroys the very reality of that object.

An artist can appreciate a painting which is complete and has a vital meaning. But Malvika, I received only a form, not the totality of a being. I cannot live with a body which is devoid of intellect. I know you will not agree, but it is impossible to find all the qualities in one person. I think one human body is not sufficient enough to hold all the human qualities one cares for. Vinnie only consists of a body, the actual qualities we left behind in your form. Just Vinnie is not enough to hold me. I cannot live with a hollow image. I always felt that marriage was an imperfect and useless institution, but it was I who committed the same stupidity a second time.

Vinnie is a separate living point. She has not accepted any defeat in life. Mere existence cannot create history. The probabiliies of the future have the capacity to do so. But I don't know what her future is going to be. As a calculative social climber she has chosen to be the mistress of a rich old man. Maybe, it will provide her the security she is looking for. Her beauty parlour was also a failure. However, I have given her an open ticket to go back to India, but occasionally what I have gathered from her is that she found India too backward and suffocating for her kind of personality. Anyway, I decided to let you know. It is precisely because I was sure she would not write to you, as she does not believe in maintaining any of her old relationships. People like you and me spend our time and energy to learn and understand from the past. Malvika please acknowledge this as my helplessness in this situation.

How are Roshan, Bhaiji, Janaki, Bedi and you? I will not forget my stay at Nirmal Kunj and all your staff, their cheerful service, their warm smiles which brightened my stay. I will come to India to meet you all. I have visited various countries and have met many people and can honestly say that I have come to the conclusion that you are unique, there is no one like you.

Yours

Pierre.'

I showed the letter to Naina. I was glad she was with me and we were about to board the bus to go to Lakhmandal. Naina read the letter and gave it back to me.

"May I tell you something, Malvika? I always felt that she would come back to you. I was half expecting to see her here when I came."

"Why?"

"Because one cannot live with the body for a long time. It refuses to give you happiness at any given time."

"Did that happen with you also Naina?"

'Yes, I survived all these years because of my ability to dance. My art kept me alive otherwise I would have been dead."

I carefully folded the letter as if it was a valuable document and kept it in my purse, which was Ma's present. I was entering an 8th or 9th century village with Naina. Why did life always take me to the past? I acknowledge the fact that the past holds me and determines my mental condition. I see myself as a hostage of the past. During the course of time, I have developed a capacity to forget whatever had happened to me, and to negate it. I had acquired an unflinching will, the will that holds me in good stead against all odds. Naina and I got down. The temple of Lakhmandal stood in front of us. There was a cave too, and the villagers believed it was the mouth of the tunnel through which the Pandavas made their escape from Varnavarta and the burning palace of wax.

Naina got busy in organising the group and talking to the people who were there to receive them. The dance was to be performed in the evening. I decided to walk towards the temple, which was not unusual. It had some carved arches and the customary roof. There were stone bulls to guard the temple. Somehow I did not feel like going inside the temple; it reminded me of Roshan's escape from reality. I walked towards the back courtyard of the temple which had a life-size male figure. I tried to decipher who it could be—was it the ruler of that time? Was it one of the Pandavas or just a simple warrior? Some people flocked in from the village. One of them asked me not to touch the figure and go back. When I asked them why, they told me, "It is a sculpture of a *Yamdoot*, the messenger of the God of death—Yama—who was invited to take the Pandavas' life but was a failure. The wax palace could not burn any of them but since he could not go back empty-handed, so he is here standing, frozen, waiting. Don't touch him, otherwise he will take you."

They laughed and I laughed with them, as I saw death monumental in its consequence, in the vision of the greatest of our seers. I sat there for sometime, thinking about death—how death separates people and ends relationships between people. Death is nothing but universal sorrow, it can be an end of a thought or ones whole consciousness.

At about seven o'clock Naina's Ballet started. A lot of villagers and a few dignitaries from nearby cities came and sat in their respective places. It was like a funfair. Naina performed various episodes from Mahabharata with her troop. The variety of characters originated from the temple, took shape and vanished. Her performance was a sort of reservoir of centuries upon centuries which came alive in front of everyone. It had everything—Kings queens, chariots, wars and death, happiness and sorrow and the final end of sorrow.

The whole performance was an eye-opener for me. I was totally engrossed. Yes, I felt that this is the reality of life. A continuous action and counter-action of various actors in a variety of roles, roles which provided them a platform of relationships. And these relationships were nothing but a trap, which prevent that individual from breathing. These relationships provide a barrier in ones normal thinking. The whole performance was a treat for the eyes. It was excellent. Naina was the only one changing clothes, masks, make-up, hair-do or even voices with a variety of expressions. There was constant background music. At that time Naina was not Naina, a woman who has suffered humiliation and pain in her past. She was an altogether different woman, changing into Radha, Rukmani, Kunti or Draupadi. She got married on the stage and she got widowed. Everything happened in such a short span. Then there was the applause. The crowd gave a standing ovation and unanimously cheered her. Naina was laughing and thanking everyone. She wanted recognition, and that was what she was getting. That is what had brought her here. She looked happy and contented. After all, she had been accepted. She was not just the Naina of the past. Each of us has an opinion about ourselves which is not self-edifying or in keeping with our status; it is a self-demanding opinion which makes life worth living.

Everything concluded, the performance over, appreciation and criticism over, Naina came back to her real self and then there was a silence...total silence. We maintained this silence throughout our journey. Some of the performers were still singing, but they dozed off due to the rythmic movement of the bus. Naina was also sleeping. I could see her face in the diffused light of the bus. Her face was without make-up, tired and worn out. She looked old and wrinkled. I calculated she must be nearly fifty-two, but with what energy she performed her dances. She could not change her childhood, her parents, her husband, her children, or her entire past—she could not do anything about it. But what was alive in her like a spark was her will to prove her existence and her desire to dance, her will of creativity. How devoted she was to her performances and that is what had changed her life. It was devotion in the true sense which helped her gain awareness in her consciousness, an awareness that was free from age, time or even space.

When we walked back, towards Nirmal Kunj, I hugged her and said, "Naina I am so happy for you. You have achieved a state of perfection through your art, and that is why you are so relaxed, energetic and vibrant."

"May I tell you Malvika, this determination is learnt from you. You were always determined to finish your studies, even if you had financial or emotional problems. You taught at that Convent. You suffered emotionally in every possible dimension in life. But you were always involved in research, research of your subject in college as well as research of your own self. I used to marvel that nothing affected you at that time, and today, when you have reached a respectable position in college, you possess 'Sewa-Ashram' instead of Nirmal Kunj. You are not there physically, yet you remain a seeker, seeking the mysteries of life.

"Well Naina, maybe you are right, but frankly I don't

want to remain a seeker, because whenever we seek, there is a division."

"Malvika, where were you, we were all so worried?" It was Roshan who came forward from Nirmal Kunj, then Bhaiji, Janaki, Manu and Bedi.

"Where did you take her Naina? We were worried where she had suddenly vanished?"

"I forgot to inform you. I thought there was no need." I felt apologetic.

Bhaiji looked relieved and promptly disappeared from the scene. Janaki took charge of Naina and Bedi also followed. Roshan stood up towering like a large flame of light at one of the entrances.

"Yes Malvika, I was worried, even though I know you don't believe in relationships."

I could not look up into his eyes, because I knew there was a change in his gaze, in his mannerism, which had no meaning for me.

I picked up Manu in my arms. Something stirred within me. I felt among all relationships there is one that does not change. This motherly instinct of my being or my relationship with this total group of people breathing under one roof of Nirmal Kunj. Yes, I am related to the total as an individual, to the creator as the created. This fundamental relationship exists for every being in this world. Bhaiji, Manu, Roshan are my alternatives. Maybe to be away from them will be the end of my fragmentation and seeking. Yes, I decided to wait for the day when these three alternatives would transform into a colourful portrait. I would wait till these pencil sketches could be coloured with all the shades of truth, to be free from the limitations of lines, identifications and roles that each one had to play.